SPARKS
FOR THE
KINDLING

SPARKS
FOR THE
KINDLING

Harold C. Bonell

The Judson Press
Valley Forge

SPARKS FOR THE KINDLING

Humbly dedicated to
PRISCILLA, MIRIAM, AND DEBORAH
who were patient under too much preaching,
encouraging when courage was low,
and are the best fruits of my ministry.

PREFACE

In the Greek legend, Prometheus was punished by the gods because he brought to man the gift of fire. By the ancients this was regarded as a divine gift only to be entrusted to the hands of the gods. When one realizes that fire is the source of man's comfort, the means by which his food is made edible, the power by which he molds the natural resources of the earth for his own use, even an instrument of destruction, it is easy to realize the awe in which the gift of fire was held.

Before modern times it became necessary sometimes for one whose fire had gone out to go to a friend or neighbor to beg a glowing coal to kindle it once again. A good friend would share his spark and enable his neighbor to start his own fire.

It is my hope that the sparks of this little volume may kindle many fires. They have begun to glow in a pastor's study as from day to day he has sought the help of the Bible. They may kindle a bit of inspiration, or flare into a flame of disagreement, or burn with steady warmth and comfort, or start a conflagration. May these few sparks start your fire.

CONTENTS

IN THE BEGINNING GOD

✓—God Is Too Big for Us
Acts 17:22-31

> The God who made the world and everything in it. . .
> does not live in shrines made by man. . . .

It is ridiculous to suppose that God, or the truth about God, is or can be encompassed completely in any religious tradition or in any religious form or place. The earth is full of the glory of God! He dwells in houses "not made with hands." Even at our best moments we but begin to touch "the hem of his garment." His knowledge "is too wonderful for me. It is high, I cannot attain it."

From the beginning of time man has been reaching toward God, seeking to understand, to realize, to behold. Man reaches his deepest understanding when he realizes his own limitation. As Pilgrim set forth upon *The Pilgrim's Progress,* Evangelist tried to help him. "Do you see yonder wicket gate?" said he. Pilgrim answered, "No." Then said the other, "Do you see yonder shining light?" He said, "I think I do." Then said Evangelist, "Keep that light in your eye, and go up directly thereto."

Our search is similar. We do not see fully what we seek, but we behold a tiny gleam of light. As we follow the gleam, we find more and more of what we seek. Wise Solomon often failed to live up to his reputation, but he showed true wisdom when he recognized that even his lavish temple could not contain God. The most glorious cathedrals on earth are not sufficient for him. Yet in temple, cathedral, and humble meetinghouse we find his presence. Where there are those who

11

with all their hearts truly seek him, they shall ever surely find him.

We not only reach for God; he is forever reaching for us. "Who goes an inch toward God, God comes a mile toward him." Heaven cannot hold him, but all of earth and all of human sin and failing cannot keep him away from us.

— God and the Grasshopper
Isaiah 40:18-24

To whom then will you liken God,
or what likeness compare with him?

If only we could see God as clearly as we see our next-door neighbor, then we could believe without reserve! How many people excuse the wavering of their faith with some such statement. How wrong can one be! When we have all our ideas of God carefully packaged, filed, and catalogued, we should throw them away. At that point we can be certain that, whatever faith we may think we have, it has lost all real significance. God is not so finite, so subject to limitation as our next-door neighbor, which is the basic reason why we cannot know him in the same way.

The prophet recognized the same problem in his time. Men tried to reduce God to a handy wood carving or a golden image. In the forty-fourth chapter of Isaiah, the prophet describes ludicrously man's attempt to make God finite. After a man cuts down a tree, ". . . he takes a part of it and warms himself, he kindles a fire and bakes bread. . . . And the rest of it he makes into a god, his idol . . . and worships it; he prays to it and says, 'Deliver me, for thou art my God!' "

God is not one of the common trivialities of life. He is not the same kind of limited reality as your fuel tank or the loaf of bread on the pantry shelf. He "sits above the circle of the earth, and its inhabitants are like grasshoppers. . . ." But man is the glorified grasshopper who can know the touch of God's

12

love, the marvel of his creation, the value of his wisdom, the demands of his justice, even though he can never reduce God to a definition or confine him to an idea.

✓ Waiting at the Gate
Psalm 24:1-10

> Lift up your heads, O gates!
> and be lifted up, O ancient doors!
> that the King of glory may come in.

The great word in modern theology is *encounter*, but here is an ancient psalm that gives evidence of a divine-human encounter before the word was used. This psalm was probably used as a sort of antiphonal anthem as pilgrims approached the holy city of Jerusalem. The approaching pilgrims would sing a line or two, and a choir on the city walls would answer them ceremoniously.

The psalm begins at the point where all true worship begins, the recognition of the greatness of God. In a world where humanity falls so far short of the family relation that should prevail, there is comfort in the fact that "The earth is the Lord's . . . the world and those who dwell therein. . . ."

However, as one contemplates the greatness of God, a very proper question must enter our thinking:

> Who shall ascend the hill of the Lord;
> And who shall stand in his holy place?

It is often necessary for us to lay aside some of the inappropriate surplus baggage if we are to get through the little postern gate that opens into the Presence. Worship is not separated from life.

To state our figure more correctly, God always waits at the gates of our lives until they can be lifted up to let the King of glory in. Too often we are laden with so much of the unnecessary and the unacceptable that we have neither will nor power to open the gate. With each new day, the chant that

13

heralds the possibility of encounter arises. "Lift up your heads, O gates . . . O doors!" The King of glory is waiting, always ready, to enter into our lives.

— God Is Not Tired of Us
Isaiah 40:27-31

The Lord is the everlasting God,
the Creator of the ends of the earth.
He does not faint or grow weary,
his understanding is unsearchable.

A mark of maturity is the ability to conceive and plan a project and to carry it through to the end. Difficulties may demand constant readjustment of details, but the mature person does not give up. The world has many dreamers who can visualize possibilities, but only the people who have stamina to persevere as they confront problems are able to change the world—to make dreams become realities.

It is not extraordinary that the Jewish nation, as portrayed in the Old Testament record, should often wonder whether God had lost interest in them. They were a people as immature as we are. When all went well, they were loud in their praise of God and eager to fulfill his purposes. But when things went badly, or when God's will seemed to be opposite to their own, they forgot their praise. In fact, they were as guilty as we are of trying to interpret God's will to undergird their own desires.

The prophet of the Second Isaiah was a man of deep insight. He was aware that God was not a wavering god of whim or fancy, however immaturely his children might act. It sounds a bit ridiculous to talk about the "maturity" of God, but "maturity" is complete fulfillment, perfection—an attribute of God. In him was conceived and is executed the plan and purpose of all things that are. The universe and those who inhabit it are not intricate toys to be set in motion

14

and forgotten. Though limited human minds change and interest lags, "He does not faint or grow weary." Through all of life we see the working of his hand.

Men of faith have a basic confidence, especially in time of human despair when the future appears dark and hope grows feeble, that God still works in wisdom, love, and justice. The prophet gives assurance that:

"He gives power to the faint, and to him
who has no might he increases strength."

Even the very mighty who would work an evil purpose are already en route to defeat, for the apparently weak shall prevail when their cause is in God.

✓ The Kindness and Severity of God
Romans 11:13-24

Note then the kindness and the severity of God: severity toward those who have fallen, but God's kindness to you, provided you continue in his kindness. . . .

One of the first verses a child learns in the church school is "God is love." It is easy to learn since it contains only three words, but it deals with a truth so profound that a lifetime does not suffice to understand it. Too often the verse is interpreted in terms of a kind of celestial Santa Claus or a doting grandfather. No matter what we do or think or are, God will work everything out happily for us in the end.

Notice that Paul did not have this concept of God. In any real understanding of love, kindness and severity unite. The parent who is all sentimental kindness, unmixed with reasonable severity, brings up a child who is not prepared for a life that shows no partiality.

In law, certain sentences are mandatory. No matter how kind a judge may be, no matter how much he may desire to make it easier for the culprit, the sentence must be served. If one has broken the law at that point, the sentence is man-

15

datory. God has established certain wise and basic laws of life. When we act according to those laws, we know life to the full, a life of challenge and opportunity, of peace and power. When we ignore or rebel against the basic laws of life, we lose touch with their Creator and suffer the consequence of the broken laws. We could experience God's kindness, but instead we sense his severity in the mandatory sentence of life.

✝ Shouts and Whispers
Psalm 19:7-14

> The law of the Lord is perfect,
> reviving the soul;
> the testimony of the Lord is sure,
> making wise the simple. . . .

"Two things fill me with . . . awe," said Immanuel Kant, the great German philosopher, "the starry heavens above me and the moral law within me." The psalmist stood humbly before these same revelations of God. "The heavens are telling the glory of God," he wrote, and "The law of the Lord is perfect, reviving the soul." A man is indeed blind who fails to see the trace of the divine hand in the majestic march of stars down the shadowed pathways of the night. However, so quietly and unobtrusively does the "law of the Lord" work within us as it gently revives the soul, that we can miss the connection with the Almighty Father.

Some easily describe the voice of human conscience as the whispering of "the sum total of all the moral, ethical, and religious" influences of one's upbringing, but there is an inexplicable plus element. The moral and religious advances of men are not defined in terms of simple training. An element of insight, of inspiration, of God periodically breaks through the established pattern of upbringing and tradition. That inner "testimony of the Lord" strangely and wonderfully "makes wise the simple."

16

The voice does not shout across the sky like the noise of thunder. It does not have the obvious power of the whirlwind, earthquake, tempest, or roaring fire. It is the whisper of the "still, small, voice"; but this, too, is the evidence of God. Listen!

+On Running Away from God
Psalm 139:1-12

> Whither shall I go from thy Spirit?
> Or whither shall I flee from thy presence?

Why should anyone try to run away from God? Most of us have spent half a lifetime trying to find him. Psalm 139 was written in a different age from ours, at a time in which God was so very real that man recognized that he was involved in everything. Man knew that he had been in the hands of God before birth when "thou didst knit me together in my mother's womb." He was assured that he would still be in the hands of God beyond death when "I ascend to heaven" or "make my bed in Sheol." When man did that which was displeasing in the sight of God, there was no place to hide.

The eternal hide-and-seek has changed through the ages. Now, like a leader in a game, we are "it." Man's ingenuity has uncovered so many secrets of our universe that we have become cocky. From birth to death we are guarded by the skill and genius made possible by the expanding comprehension of man. Although we have much knowledge, we are in danger of losing the greatest secret of the universe, that of the constant awareness of God. We might wish to change the old Psalm to "Whither shall I go [to find] thy Spirit? Or [how can I enter into] thy presence?"

Many of us, for all our guilty consciences, would rather run to God for assurance than run from him in shame or fear. We need the restoration of our confidence. Although God does not change, our ideas about him do. Nevertheless, he is still beside us in the heaven of our highest hope or in the hell of our deepest despair, in the darkness of our doubt or in the bright light of our clearest understanding, in the miracle of birth or in the mystery of death. He is near us at home in the midst of our loved ones or in the uttermost parts of the sea or space when we are strangers and alone. Such knowledge is too wonderful even for our present ingenuity, but he searches for us and knows us always.

THOU ART THE CHRIST

⌐ Christian Identification
Matthew 11:2-15

"Are you he who is to come, or shall we look for another?"

John was having difficulties with some religious doubts. He had staked everything on his faith that Jesus was the Christ. Now, in the discouragement and frustration that naturally accompanies an unjust sentence, he found himself questioning. It may be that, in keeping with ancient messianic expectations, he expected Jesus to assert himself quickly and to destroy the enemies of God and goodness. Had John made a mistake in his appraisal of the Man from Nazareth? Somehow, by way of the prison grapevine, he got word to one of his disciples. "Ask Jesus," he said, "whether he is truly the answer to our prayers. Or will God send someone else?"

Jesus answered in a way that even we can understand. "Tell John what you hear and see: The blind receive their sight," he said, "and the lame walk; lepers are cleansed and the deaf hear; the dead are raised up, and the poor have good news preached to them." Do not be blinded by the miraculous elements in this catalog of good works. Jesus usually did not depend on miracles to prove his authority. What he was saying basically was, "The forgotten of earth are no longer forgotten." This was an authentic religious revolution.

We hear many challenges to faith in our time. Men are condemned for believing this or for not believing that. The Master said once, "By their fruits ye shall know them." Those who are more interested in condemning than in redeeming would have been very uncomfortable with Jesus of Nazareth. "By this shall all men know that you are my disciples," he said, "if you have love one for another." He expressed his love for others in acts that made their lives more abundant. All the words by which we express our faith have little meaning unless we follow the example of Jesus Christ who remembered the forgotten, redeemed the lost, and loved the sinner.

✝What's in a Name?
Matthew 1:18-25

. . . and you shall call his name Jesus, for he will save his people from their sins.

Does your name have a meaning? The ancients did not choose a name simply because it sounded good or had been the name of a favorite uncle. The Scriptures have many stories of children whose names were given to express a conviction of their parents or a special hope for the child. The Gospel of Matthew indicates that Jesus' name was given as a result of Joseph's dream. The name "Jesus" is derived from the Hebrew word meaning "God is salvation." The Child of Bethlehem was so named because, as the Gospel states, "He will save his people from their sins."

Because this was the master purpose of his life, it needs careful definition. Generations of Christian thinkers have labored long with the "Savior" concept of Jesus and have produced various theories of the atonement that give meaning to his name. Some notions of atonement make God a stern and rigid judge caught in the mesh of his own unrelenting justice. Some make him a medieval king more concerned with his own honor than with the welfare of a culprit. Some give up the idea of God's love in order to safeguard what they are pleased to call his justice.

The Gospel reveals a Jesus who was both simple and profound in his teaching. He made no effort to save men from the *consequences* of their sin, to step between cause and effect. He sought to save them from the *power* of their sins. Men were subject to their own pride and selfishness; Jesus called them to a kingdom of God where they would be subject to God alone. In the life and teaching of Jesus, God has revealed his purpose for man. When man gives his ultimate loyalty to Christ, then he is free from his bondage to sin. He is completely at one with his God, and this is atonement.

† When Men See God
John 1:1-16

Neighbor

> No one has ever seen God; the only Son, who is in the bosom of the Father, he has made him known.

There was once a time when God moved in next door and became the near neighbor of everyone who would have him. But even when he lived next door there were but a few who recognized him.

A wise friend of mine once called Christmas the feast of the "neighborliness of God." John was dealing with this same basic concept when he wrote, "And the Word became flesh and dwelt among us. . . ." Although this idea was much more familiar to the Gnostic philosophy of his day than it is in our time, we also can find in his illustration a vivid truth. All that men had ever tried to do in explaining God in words and ideas was most completely accomplished in the life and teaching of Jesus Christ. God's grace and glory, his truth and fullness became known in him.

To use a different figure of speech, the family resemblance was so clear in Jesus that, in the Son, men saw the Father. Of course there were those who failed to note the resemblance. "He came to his own home, and his own people received him not." But some recognized their new neighbor, and "to all who received him, and believed in his name, he gave power to become children of God."

21

The good Neighbor moved away, but the neighborhood has never lost his influence. He left behind a spirit of confidence and awareness so vivid that it is the breath of life to all who know him. When one encounters those experiences of challenging joy, disturbing doubt, overwhelming grief, shattering temptation, the experiences where he always helped, we become aware that he has never really gone but is always beside us.

✓ Jesus the Disturber
Mark 11:15-19

> . . . and he overturned the tables of the moneychangers and the seats of those who sold pigeons. . . .

Jesus was always upsetting something, and the upset still continues. Many teachings of the Master are comforting. The Gospels include stories in which he quieted fears, healed diseases, and solved personal problems. Yet, he disturbed men deeply. He shook the carefully guarded tree of their lives until the rotten fruit dropped off and the blossoms of a new spring had a chance to develop. Jesus comforted the disturbed and disturbed the comfortable.

The money-changers of the Temple and the sellers of sacrifices probably thought quite highly of themselves as being necessary and important adjuncts to the religious services of the Temple. If they made a profit in the process, how gracious was God that he had put them in such an advantageous place! They slipped into the easy rationalization of which we too are guilty when we justify what we want to do in spite of gnawing questions that will not be silent within us.

Even though he did not urge such a system upon his followers, Jesus was not deliberately destroying the old sacrificial system. He was upsetting a false standard of values that existed even in the shadow of the Temple. He was disturbing all smug, self-satisfied formalism that waters faith down to a tradition and reduces worship to a ritual. What does the Master upset in you?

—For This Purpose
John 12:20-26

> Truly, truly, I say to you, unless a grain of wheat falls into the earth and dies, it remains alone; but if it dies, it bears much fruit.

When life has a mission that is big enough, death loses all its power to frighten or even to mystify. John's Gospel adds a few details to the account of Jesus' triumphal entry into Jerusalem en route to the cross. These give us a little fuller concept of Jesus' sense of mission.

The Pharisees had just complained that "the world has gone after him." As if to underline that fact, the Gospel writer added at this point the record of the coming of Greek proselytes who, approaching Philip and Andrew, said, "We wish to see Jesus." Here was the fulfillment of the Master's hope. Never had he withheld the truth from any man because of nationality, race, or previous religious conviction. Here was the breaking of the barrier! Through him now the love of God could be revealed to all the world! This was indeed the hour "for the son of man to be glorified."

Yes, Jesus knew what this meant. Those who opposed him would be content only with his death. Should he turn back on his new opportunity? "No, for this purpose I have come to this hour. Father, glorify thy name."

In his courage, devotion, and deep insight were the marks of his divinity. Here was the Master of men making a great choice. He was not a pawn in the divine hand but a Son of the divine love.

Death is the great "bogey man" of the ages. But when death is just an incident in one's confident fulfillment of the will of God, it loses its terror. The seed is planted, but the harvest is assured.

✝ How Much for Your Whistle?
Romans 3:9-26

> . . . since all have sinned and fall short of the glory of God, they are justified by his grace as a gift, through the redemption which is in Christ Jesus.

A great problem with man is that he sells out too easily and too cheaply. The account of Jesus' temptation is, on a grand scale, the story of what happens in lesser lives with weaker sales resistance. Constant bids are offered to all of us by which we hope to buy happiness, power, prestige, security, or all of those other things for which men live and die.

Benjamin Franklin, in *Poor Richard's Almanac,* tells a story of his childhood. He had been given, on some special occasion, a sum of money that he took immediately to a toy store. There he found a whistle that pleased him so much that he emptied his pockets and gave his entire small fortune for it. When he came home and blew it about the house, his cousins laughed at him for his poor bargain. Their ridicule cost him more shame and embarrassment than his whistle gave him pleasure. From that time onward he lived on the principle, "Do not pay too much for your whistle."

How often we sell our souls for a whistle that brings more irritation than satisfaction! All have stumbled and fallen short of the glory that God has built potentially within us, but God looks on us with more compassion than we deserve. He sent Jesus Christ to *buy us back* from the bad bargains we have made. That is the basic meaning of *redemption.* When we know the price that Jesus paid, how can we ever sell out again?

24

The Bond of Life
Colossians 2:8-19

For in him the whole fulness of deity dwells bodily, and you have come to fulness of life in him, who is the head of all rule and authority.

Let us not assume that the freedom of religion implies that anyone can believe anything he wants to believe and call it religion. Religious faith should call forth the best of individual thinking, but it has reference to an *object* of faith as well as to an individual's relation to and thought about that *object*.

There are various threats to the freedom of religion. One comes from the person who attempts individually or institutionally to impose on all persons his regulations and interpretations, as if they had the authority of God. The opposite extreme is born out of a desire to escape any concept or discipline that might become discomforting or inconvenient. So the difficult matters of faith are belittled, and compromise becomes the rule.

True religion is a strong bond that has its anchor beyond man. Life, to be secure, must have a relationship beyond itself. The Man of Nazareth demonstrated the steadiness of a life that is firmly moored. He was free to be himself because he was so strongly bound to God. No man is really free unless he is bound to something that is bigger than he is. Paul warned the Christians of Colossae to hold ". . . fast to the Head from whom the whole body, nourished and knit together through its joints and ligaments, grows with a growth that is from God."

FRUIT OF THE SPIRIT

/

⊥The Shining Spirit
Exodus 34:29-35

Moses did not know that the skin of his face shone
because he had been talking with God.

To be in the presence of God does things to people. The
writers of the book of the Exodus made this point very con-
cretely. The shining face of Moses, the man who had been
with God, frightened the irresponsible mob of people whom
he was leading.

We are not aware of the shining of the skin of a man's face,
but we soon become aware of the shining of his spirit. A news-
paperman in Boston once reported a gray and unpleasant
day, but he added, "Phillips Brooks walked down Washing-
ton Street, and the sun shone." This is not the description
of that obnoxious Pollyanna type of person who always
forces a smile or makes a tritely cheerful comment. Phillips
Brooks, in his capacity as a pastor, must have been exposed
to as much human heartache as any man in Boston, but he
was a man who had been with God. For this reason, not because of any artificial struggle to be cheerful, he was a shining
personality.

The truly shining spirit usually does not know that he
shines. His is a reflected glory. He is like a bit of fluorescent
mineral which soaks up the light so completely that it continues to glow in the darkness. Each man, if he dares, can
expose himself to the perfect Light to become that kind of
shining spirit who makes the sun to shine even when days
are darkest.

26

— Shared Experience
Mark 1:21-34

> They were astonished at his teaching, for he taught them
> as one who had authority, and not as the scribes.

Religion is not taught or learned—it is experienced. It consists of a deep awareness of God that gives meaning to our lives. Evil is known as evil because one is aware of the everlasting goodness against which it stands. Goodness becomes desirable because it is recognized as participating in the only true Reality in the universe. Life has significance because it can partake of a certain eternal quality that does not wear out in the limits of our threescore years and ten.

But, even if religion is primarily an experience, it is still true that much can be taught or learned to enrich that experience and to make it more deeply meaningful. Ideas, forms, symbols, and even activities, so much in disrepute among theologians, can make a rich experience more real and penetrating.

Teachers of religion have sought to provide such enrichment of experience for their disciples through the ages. Sometimes they have borrowed from others what they have not experienced themselves to pass on to their students. Such teaching becomes a mechanical process of transferring a load of supplies from one vehicle to another. The new vehicle might receive something useful, but not necessarily because of the one who made the transfer.

The astonishment called forth by the great Teacher came from the fact that he shared his own life and experience with his disciples. His was not a transfer of supplies but a transfusion of life. What he taught he taught not because someone else had told him but because he had tried it out in the living experiment of his own experience. As the living truth of the Teacher's life poured into the lives of his faithful disciples, their lives became vibrantly new, empowered by the transfusion.

✓ Spiritual Responsibility
John 14:12-17, 25-31

> . . . the Counselor, the Holy Spirit, whom the Father
> will send in my name, he will teach you all things, and
> bring to your remembrance all that I have said to you.

Jesus used a vivid Greek word to describe the Holy Spirit. In some of our old hymns it was anglicized without translation into the word *paraclete,* which is derived from the Greek *"para"* and *"kaleo,"* meaning "alongside" and "I call." This meaning pictures one who walks at your side at all times to steady you with encouragement and the touch of a firm hand. In the King James version of the Scriptures it is translated "Comforter," but we have so misused the word "comfort" that it has lost its real meaning. For us comfort often means a gentle pat on the head, cushioned ease, the avoiding of anything difficult. "Comfort" is derived from the Latin *"cum,"* meaning "with," and *"fortis,"* meaning "strength."

While Jesus walked with his disciples, quite naturally they leaned heavily upon him and his guidance. When a problem arose, he was the source of a special wisdom derived from his insight into the will of God.

Following his leadership was like riding through heavy traffic with a skillful driver at the wheel. We might know the rules of the road, the signs and symbols that must be observed, and even the possible penalties if we do not obey. But this is not entirely our problem, because someone else is doing the driving. Today, however, Jesus' disciples must walk in their own strength and act by the wisdom of their own insight into God's will. Like driving a car—when we hold the wheel, we are personally responsible to observe the regulations. Red light or green speaks directly to us. It is our individual responsibility to maintain right relations with the authorities in charge. We pay the penalty ourselves if we fail.

Similarly, the disciple is responsible when the teacher leaves him on his own. The same purpose must be served, the same precepts are true, the same power is available; but the responsibility rests with the disciple, not the teacher. Also, now the Spirit speaks to us directly, and we must respond.

✝ Empowered by the Spirit
Galatians 6:1-10

> Brethren, if a man is overtaken in any trespass, you who are spiritual should restore him in a spirit of gentleness.

One of the major virtues of the Christian faith is the virtue of being able to forgive. Indeed, the Christian obligation goes beyond forgiveness for an evil done to the responsibility for redeeming the individual from the power of his evil. But Alexander Pope's epigram is still true, "To err is human, to forgive divine." We are too willing to leave all forgiveness to God and to excuse our harbored grudges with an easy, "We are only human."

The apostle Paul did not excuse Christians so easily. "You who are spiritual [empowered by the Spirit of God]," he said, "should restore him [the trespasser] with gentleness."

In wartime Germany many automobiles were converted to a kind of wood-burning engine. The equipment was faulty and inefficient, causing all kinds of difficulty. When the motor would not work at all, it was helpful to get a powerful push from some neighbor who, because of official connections, had a good car with an efficient, dependable, gasoline engine.

The Christian is empowered by a source of power that never fails. He should get behind his brother in his lapses and give him the firm and gentle push that will give a new start. This obligation becomes even greater when the Christian remembers how often he has stalled and needed the same push.

—The Highway in the Heart
Psalm 84:1-12

> Blessed are the men whose strength is in thee,
> in whose heart are the highways to Zion.

Religious devotion can be on different levels. Some people seem deeply devoted to God as long as they are healthy, wealthy, and wise enough to assume that God is being very good to them. Such religion has sometimes been known to fail when adversity comes. In wartime another level of religious devotion is characterized by the name of "foxhole religion." This is marked by an intense interest in God and devotion to him when circumstances are obviously beyond human control—and death is imminent. "Foxhole religion" often has no lasting quality, though, when the emergency has passed.

Another kind of religion, however, builds a life on the foundation of a devoted search for God, an honest recognition of his supreme worth (worship), and a faithful concern for the doing of his will. In such a person the soul "longs, yea, faints for the courts of the Lord." Though he is busy with the earning of a living, or the circumstances of life take him far from his customary place of worship, in his heart "are the highways to Zion." Nothing stands between him and his service to the Almighty. Though he must pass through the desolate "Valley of Baca," he is scarcely aware of its desolation. It becomes for him "a place of springs" because it leads toward an opportunity to serve his God. He would prefer a single day spent in devoted service with an awareness of God's presence about him than a thousand days spent at any other task. For him it would mean more to be a doorkeeper in God's house than to dwell as an honored guest in the most lavish tent of wickedness. For such a man, God is the very sun that gives him life and the shield that keeps him secure.

The phraseology of this ancient psalm is obsolete in our world, but the spirit of it is timeless. The awareness of God and the sense of our relationship to him are still the elements that give meaning to life in a world where life so often loses its meaning.

+ Price Tags
Acts 8:14-24

> Now when Simon saw that the Spirit was given through the laying on of the apostles' hands, he offered them money. . . .

There is a constant tendency to think that anything can be bought if one can pay a high enough price. Simon of Samaria thought that he could even buy the gifts of the Holy Spirit. Maybe he hoped that he could possess the gift of healing that had been made evident in the lives of the apostles. It is a worthy gift and much to be desired, but there are no short cuts to obtain it. To be able to perform any great act of human service normally takes discipline, study, and years of experience.

Think how many gifts of the Spirit are given to us without material cost! There is an old saying, "The best things in life are free." This is especially true of the good gifts of the Spirit. Of course they require another kind of price—the price of commitment to the will of God, receptivity to his guidance, and faithfulness in his service. No wealth can buy the gifts of the Spirit nor can they be denied to those in most dire poverty. At this point Dives and Lazarus are equal.

Live, then, in patience to let the Spirit flow through your life into the life of the world. It flows in as the grace, the free gift of God; but from the faithful it flows forth into the world as love, joy, peace, patience, kindness, goodness, faithfulness, gentleness, and self-control. Maybe these are greater miracles than the gift of healing, and all these are beyond all price.

___My Father's Son
Romans 8:1-17

> When we cry, "Abba! Father!" it is the Spirit himself bearing witness with our spirit that we are children of God. . . .

Man is in great disrepute in our time. The anguish and barbarism of war and all its accompanying inhumanities have destroyed man's confidence in himself. When confidence becomes conceit it should be destroyed, but never let the evil in the world blind us to the fact that God is still working through man to accomplish his divine purpose.

The old Quaker insight that recognizes something of God in every man must not be lost in the present emphasis upon man's hopelessness. Paul was deeply aware of the sinfulness of human nature, but he was also aware that God's spirit worked even through that human nature. We reach out of our confusion and weakness to grasp the Father's hand, but it is his spirit within us that prompts our reaching.

When the prodigal son had reached the lowest depth of his degradation, it must have been his greatest comfort to know that he was still his father's son. Even in his shame and frustration, he had confidence in his father's love and understanding. Could any fact of our nature ever mean so much to us as the fact that we are children of God? Let us, then, cultivate the family resemblance that will let those who look upon us know who is our Father.

THE MEANING OF LIFE

— The Meaning of Man
Genesis 2:4-8

> Then the Lord God formed man of dust from the ground, and breathed into his nostrils the breath of life; and man became a living being.

The Book of Genesis tells the story of creation twice, but the second telling is the more dramatic. Even before these words were written, men must have been asking what man's place in the universe might be. To such a question many answers have been given. In this account of creation man is but a handful of dust scooped up by God from some ancient river bottom. Into this bit of dust God "breathed . . . the breath of life." At the opposite extreme, the poet of the eighth Psalm murmurs in awe, "What is man, that thou art mindful of him. . . . For thou hast made him little lower than the angels" (King James Version), or, as one translator dares to put it, "little less than God!"

What is man, then? A little higher than the dust or a little lower than God? The question is not quite so bewildering if we add one and one and get man plus God. God can take the dust of the earth and make it a little lower than the angels.

There is a great difference between origins and destinations. Man does not lift himself from dust to divinity by his own bootstraps. Sometimes, in humility, he is wise enough to place his tiny handful of dust in the hand of God. Then God can breathe into that dust a life that is beyond all human imagining.

The story of creation ends in the tragic tale of man's dis-

33

obedience, of his failure to yield to the will of his Creator. Much has been made of this part of the human story through the years. However, the story of Scripture and of humanity reaches a climax far beyond that. It climbs to the glorious record of that One whose human dust was most completely in the hand of God and, so, was the only begotten Son of God. He yielded most completely and showed what man can be.

✓ Imitating God
Ephesians 4:25—5:2

> Therefore be imitators of God, as beloved children. And walk in love, as Christ loved us and gave himself up for us. . . .

It has been said that the most sincere flattery is imitation. But who would ever use the word "flattery" to describe a relationship to God? Yet there have been times when men seem to have assumed that God would yield to their flattery in much the same way that a weak human being yields. Paul says nothing to the churches in the area of Ephesus about flattery, but he clearly describes the process of imitation.

How can one imitate God who moves in such a "mysterious way"? When he calls Christians to "be imitators of God," he holds Christ before them as the great example. Thomas à Kempis once said: "He who follows me can never walk in darkness, our Lord says. Here are words of Christ, words of warning; if we want to see our way truly, never a trace of blindness left in our hearts, it is his life, his character, we must take for our model." Paul places a finger upon actual acts and attitudes that are a part of such imitation, the speaking of truth, the control of anger, guarding the tongue, willingness for reconciliation, simple kindness, the forgiving spirit. These are part of the imitation of God as we know him through Jesus Christ our Lord.

Do not be shocked with the notion that such a call to imitation implies the possibility of our attaining the ultimate perfection that we commonly attribute only to God. The practiced eye quickly distinguishes the imitation from the real, but the imitation can also be great in its own right. God is far beyond our complete understanding, but he has given to us the great Example through whom we find it possible to imitate him.

⌐The Choice Is Ours
Romans 6:12-23

The wages of sin is death, but the free gift of God is eternal life in Christ Jesus our Lord.

Life is infinitely more than eating and sleeping and breathing. It must have some meaning and interest and significance for the person who lives it to make life worth the effort of all the eating and sleeping and breathing.

Death is not simply the stopping of physical functioning. Some who walk among us with every physical function in order are dead, for they do not even know the real meaning of life.

Sin is the deliberate choosing to devote the good gift of life that God has given to us to those activities that have no lasting meaning or permanent quality. That kind of stubborn, human conceit will not be guided in any other direction even if it means abundant life. It is the living death of knowing what life could be but of always falling short. It is like the pain of a curable disease that we suffer continually because we will not take a doctor's advice or follow his direction. If, at long last, we yield and place ourselves trustingly in the physician's care, we can be cured and can live in good health once more.

The Good Physician patiently waits until we turn to him. Then does he give us the free gift of a life of such quality that we cannot imagine it.

✛ Peace in Our Time
Romans 5:1-11

> Since we are justified by faith, we have peace with God
> through our Lord Jesus Christ.

It was Augustine who said, "Thou hast made us for thyself,
O Lord, and our hearts are restless until they rest in Thee."
His statement came out of his own long restlessness and
struggle with God's will before he finally stopped depending
upon himself and turned to God.

Life is often like the struggle of a person learning how to
swim. He makes frantic efforts to keep himself afloat. Arms
and legs thrash wildly about, and he succeeds only in sinking
when he would swim. Then comes the moment when he dis-
covers that the very buoyancy of the water keeps him afloat,
not his struggle. He lets himself go, and, with the natural
motions that are intended to make the most of that buoyancy,
he floats with ease, and all his fear is gone.

So do we struggle with life and our world, as if our efforts
were the deciding factor, but "There's a wideness in God's
mercy like the wideness of the sea," and there is a buoyancy
in his love that supports us now and always if we will let it.
Only when we discover this, do we find the peace that is not
freedom from all of life's problems, but assurance and confidence in the face of all circumstances.

— Unashamed
Romans 1:8-17

> For I am not ashamed of the gospel.

I once belonged to a club that had an unwritten law for-
bidding its members to discuss politics or religion. It was assumed that these two major subjects represented potentially

divisive elements in a group of men of widely differing opinions. The net result was the frequent infringement of the "unwritten law"; or, when the members obeyed it, of hours of time wasted in discussing nonentities.

Some people cannot speak of their religious faith without becoming domineering or belligerent. Such attitudes are usually the confession of a weak and uncertain faith, fearful lest some opposing idea may overturn it.

The great saints and seers of religion had no need for defending their faith nor for forcing it upon others. It was so real to them that no power could destroy it. It was so evident to those about that it became as contagious as a communicable disease.

Too often in our time we become red-faced with embarrassment even to speak of religious matters, lest someone become offended or think we are unduly pious. We need the assurance of Paul who said simply, "I am not ashamed of the gospel." The same gospel is the foundation of our faith. Without shame or embarrassment, let us confess it.

✝ Who Is in Charge?
Romans 7:13-25

> I do not do the good I want, but the evil I do not want is what I do. . . . Who will deliver me from this body of death? Thanks be to God through Jesus Christ our Lord!

Who is the boss in your house? I do not mean in your family, but in the household of your individual life? Can you make your own decisions and see them through, or do you have Paul's problem?

Even when he determined to do good or to be good, he found himself falling short on many occasions. When he built up his defenses against evil, he found them crumbling where he least expected. We find ourselves so continually in the same predicament that we can sympathize. We excuse ourselves in our failures. We rationalize in the face of every obstacle.

Hall Caine once wrote a novel entitled *The Bondman* based upon the symbolic struggle of a man who constantly faced defeat. At last he wrestled, like Jacob of old, with his opponent until he could pin him down and look into his face. He found himself staring into the familiar features of his own countenance, for he was his own greatest opponent.

Paul realizes this struggle with his own human nature and shouts in despair, "Who will deliver me from this body of death?" Moffatt translates the next verse with the simple affirmation, "God will!" When we cease struggling for ourselves with ourselves and, instead, wrestle with self and the world for God, life begins to become a victory and not a defeat.

⌒ Doubt and Faith
John 20:24-29

> "Have you believed because you have seen me? Blessed are those who have not seen and yet believe."

Thomas made himself famous by his doubt. It was no disgrace that he wanted to be shown. He has had plenty of companionship through the ages. Religion has been hindered more than it has been helped by blind faith. God expects a man to use his mind as well as his heart. Jesus did not scold Thomas for his insistence but quietly met his demands, and, as a result, Thomas no longer needed to make the test.

Thomas stubbed his toe on the same stumbling blocks that stand in our way. He easily assumed that anything he could not understand could not exist. He discovered that:

... no eye has seen, nor ear heard,

nor the heart of man conceived

what God has prepared for those who love him.

Do not assume that the limits of your understanding mark the limits of possibility.

In the second place, he assumed that material proof was necessary to the undergirding of a spiritual truth. Too often we speak of physical man as having a soul or spirit. Actually, we should recognize that it is quite the other way around. Spiritual man has, and is sometimes hindered by, a body. Stigmata can be counterfeited. The material does not prove the spiritual. To touch the wounds would have been no real proof of the fact that "death no longer has dominion over him."

No man has yet been able to grasp the mystery of man completely, and certainly not the mystery of God. Use the best thinking that God has made possible for you. Then, "Blessed are those who have not seen and yet believe."

— Answering Back to God
Romans 9:19-26

"Who are you, a man, to answer back to God? Will what is molded say to its molder, 'Why have you made me thus?'"

The hymn writer sings, "God moves in a mysterious way his wonders to perform." Because the mystery of God's way is so far beyond our comprehension, it is not difficult to slip into the habit of being critical even of God. Of course we are seldom bold enough to give outward expression to such criticism. But, deep within, we catch ourselves thinking, "Why did God do such a thing?" or even, "If I were God, this is not what I would do."

Paul, in this passage, is handling some of the most profound mysteries of God's dealing with man. He is well aware of the petulant questions that arise in the minds of his readers. We seldom plunge so deeply into such theological speculation, but, even closer to the surface, we can find many more questions than we can answer. Why has God made us as we are, limited in so many ways, prone to error, hindered by so many human frailties, if he expects us to be useful to him?

It is as if the molded clay began to talk back to the potter. How patient is the divine Potter whose gentle hand continues our molding, in spite of our childish complaints, until we reach at last a form of usefulness! Only then do we realize the "wonders" accomplished by God's "mysterious way."

✓How to Win
Judges 7:1-8

"The people with you are too many for me to give the Midianites into their hand, lest Israel vaunt themselves against me, saying, 'My own hand has delivered me.'"

Gideon's story is one of the heroic ones of ancient Israel. Like so many before and after him, he resisted the call of God upon his life. When, at last, he accepted his task, he did it with all his might. The great event of Gideon's story gives us an interesting insight into the significance of majorities and minorities.

He started with a great army, but he reduced it to a few. First he sent home those who were afraid. Fear is an infectious disease, and a cause is poorly served by those who live by it. Not only are they well nigh useless in themselves, but they also destroy the morale of those who would dare.

Secondly, Gideon tested his remaining men to see if they could keep their minds upon the job at hand. Most of them failed. One of the marks of maturity is the ability to start a task and to see it through to completion without letting anything else distract. The "attention span" of the modern adult is distressingly brief. We live in a time when we must create continually new slogans, new symbols in the endless effort to keep the minds of men and women on the service of some great cause in which they have taken only the first steps.

Finally, Gideon took his tiny remaining army and gave them a confident war cry, "The sword of the Lord and of

Gideon." Although the sword has been placed too often in the hand of the Lord as if it belonged there, we should remember Gideon's was a primitive time in the childhood of the race. Gideon advanced in the name of the Lord. What a difference it would make for us to serve our countless causes in the name of the Lord. Some causes would not be great enough to justify that name, and we would have to discard them. For the worthy remainder, such faith guarantees a victory. If such confidence cannot be a part of your great service, find a new cause!

— The Margin of Difference
Matthew 5:13-20

". . . unless your righteousness exceeds that of the scribes and Pharisees, you will never enter the kingdom of heaven."

Christians are supposed to be noticeably different from those who make no profession of Christian faith, but are they? Bishop Brent, the great missionary leader of the Philippines, once sadly summed up a visit to the United States by saying, "The tragedy is that Christians are not sufficiently different from non-Christians."

This does not imply a "holier-than-thou" attitude. It means that when one embraces the Christian way he is as completely changed as if he had dyed his face green! Actually, something much more radical has happened—something which in no way is superficial. He has changed the basic motivation of life from that of satisfying himself to that of willing the will of God.

T. R. Glover appraised the triumph of the early church in the face of the Roman Empire. When he asked, "How did the Church do it?" he answered his own question quickly: "If I may invent or adopt three words, the Christian 'out-lived' the pagan, 'out-died' him, and 'out-thought' him." This is essentially Jesus' emphasis when he says, ". . . unless your righteousness exceeds that of the scribes and Pharisees."

A Christian who has lost his sense of dedication so that he seeks to be a Christian on a minimum basis is as worthless as salt that has lost its taste. The Christian who really lives his beliefs in Christ stands out like a city on a hill, or a candle on a candlestick.

— Freedom to Forgive
Philemon 4-14

. . . I preferred to do nothing without your consent in order that your goodness might not be by compulsion but of your own free will.

Paul expected that a man who bore the name of Christian would act like one. One of the key proofs of Christian character is the ability to forgive. Paul could have used his prestige as a recognized leader of the church to demand forgiveness of Philemon, but virtue on command is not virtue at all.

Onesimus, a young slave from the household of Philemon, had sought out Paul in Rome. Apparently he confessed that he had run away and, possibly, even carried away with him something of value. Paul put both the slave and the master to the test. He sent Onesimus back to risk the possibility of serious punishment and to beg the pardon of the master. He sent this letter, preserved for us in Scripture, to give the master the opportunity to show that his Christian faith was not simply words but the complete commitment of a life.

What would your reaction be to such a letter that challenged so daringly the authenticity of your faith? We have moved, thank God, beyond the institution of slavery, but we shall never move beyond the need for learning the hard lesson of how to forgive. When we are guilty of having wronged another, we, like Onesimus, owe it to our Master to make amends, but we can never command forgiveness. When we have been wronged, we have the chance for the greater testimony of forgiving, as God forgives us, not "by compulsion but of your own free will."

✝ The Lonely Struggle
Genesis 32:22-32

> And Jacob was left alone; and a man wrestled with him until the breaking of the day.

Jacob spent most of his life wrestling. He was a "status seeker" of another day. He struggled to assume the position of head of the family, even though that honor properly belonged to his brother Esau. Like most people who are continually trying to climb to a place of prestige that does not come naturally to them, he was never quite satisfied.

If he was a worthy ancestor of the Hebrew people, there must have been times when his conscience troubled him. It is significant that at the great turning point of his life, he was left alone. Our biggest decisions are always lonely ones. He had sent his flocks and herdsmen and even his family ahead of him, hoping that his angry brother might be calmed by their intervention, that his wrath would not last until he met Jacob.

So he was left alone, but he discovered that a man with a problem is never alone. God was so certainly at the place of Jacob's greatest struggle that, when it was over, he could only say, "I have seen God face to face." In our own great decisions, our personal battles of right and wrong, as well as our individual facing of deserved consequences, we are always left alone. Then, when we have finally made the decision, we know that our struggle was with God himself, that we have seen him face to face.

Tongue Trouble
James 3:1-12

> . . . the tongue is a little member and boasts of great things. How great a forest is set ablaze by a small fire!

Even the saints had tongue trouble. There are scriptural records of hasty speaking on the part of Peter. James and John certainly did not think things through before they asked for places of honor in the kingdom. Thomas must have regretted his expressions of doubt when he met the risen Lord.

The Epistle of James speaks of teachers' responsibility in the use of their tongues. It is possible to speak as gospel truth something that is only human error. We may use the tongue to boast and curse—surely it is "a restless evil, full of deadly poison." We are aware of the hasty tongue, the lying tongue, the angry tongue. "How great a forest is set ablaze by a small fire!"

Yet we are only using a figure of speech. The tongue is but a small member under higher control. Like an index tab on a filing folder, it tells what is within. The tongue reveals a mind, a spirit, and an attitude that may attempt to dominate everyone or may be entirely considerate of others' hopes, feelings, and opinions. It indicates a self under control or out of control. It shows a person who selfishly seeks only his own advantage, or one who serves the Lord.

A careless tongue is a fire that can destroy vast, green forests of goodwill which were cultivated by years, or even generations, of thoughtfulness—and new forests grow slowly. A disciplined tongue is a well-handled rudder that can guide the ship of a great purpose through the greatest storm. That tongue of yours is wonderful and dangerous. Guard it and guide it well.

√Sorting Out Our Values
Genesis 25:27-34

Esau said, "I am about to die; of what use is a birthright to me?"

It is not difficult for one to make a good appraisal of the true values of life when one is simply philosophizing. Most of us know what is good, true, and right and can distinguish it from what is bad, false, and wrong. But life seldom works out so simply that our neat little categories show their labels clearly when we are in the midst of living. We find ourselves thinking of all the extenuating circumstances. What is good at this time? What is true in this situation? What is right for these people?

If you had chatted with Esau on a calm Sabbath afternoon when he was comfortably full and well rested, he would have told you that his birthright — his privilege and responsibility as a slightly elder son — was very dear to him. But Jacob talked to him in a different situation.

Esau was not really about to die; he simply exaggerated a minor problem into major proportions, as we often do. He used it as a good excuse to forget his true sense of values. He said, "I'm starved to death! Who cares for a birthright? I want to eat!" We too are always tempted to lose our sense of the eternal in the face of the immediate. It is important to be able to sort out the absolute from the relative values.

Some things in life are so important that circumstances cannot change them. Faith is one of them, and real love is another. Sometimes we are tempted to deal with these as Esau dealt with his birthright, but they are of God and allow us to partake of his stability and invariability.

⊕ On Keeping House
Luke 10:38-42

"Martha, Martha, you are anxious and troubled about many things; one thing is needful."

Martha, the busy housekeeper, has aroused more sympathy through nineteen centuries than almost any other character in the New Testament. Countless busy women have looked askance at Mary, seated calmly at Jesus' feet while her sister bustled about the tasks of hospitality.

There is a time for hospitality and all that it entails. Home would be a little less than home without the ministry of careful hands, the blessed sisterhood of pots and pans, of brooms and dustcloths. Sitting at the feet, even of the Master, peels no potatoes and makes no beds. Kipling looks on the scene with tongue in cheek as he chides the sons of Mary. "They have cast their burden upon the Lord, and the Lord, He lays it on Martha's sons!"

Much can be said for faithful Martha and all her numerous offspring. However, in our sympathy for Martha, let us not lose the meaning of Mary. One can become so involved in the "nasty neatness" of the routine of home or business that the great opportunities are missed, or the supreme necessities overlooked. The warm companionship of children, the comradeship of home, the awareness of someone else's "great event" can be lost in the necessity for keeping to a slavish schedule. The vision of a great purpose, the fellowship of a common service, even the renewal of a moment of quiet, can smother under the pressure of always keeping house.

✛ Listening
I Samuel 3:1-10

> Therefore Eli said to Samuel, "Go, lie down; and if he calls you, you shall say, 'Speak, Lord, for thy servant hears.'"

It is not easy to recognize a voice, especially when other voices are calling. Quite naturally, Samuel assumed what he heard was the voice of Eli when it was really the voice of God. The great problem in life is to make the distinction.

Many things work against us. We are distracted by the many voices which call to us. Many of them are sweet and gentle voices calling us to worthy enterprises. It is easy to mistake the good for the best. What is even more bewildering is our own voice within us which is tuned to our self-seeking, our search for ease, our avoidance of discomfort and inconvenience—until we lose the voice of God in the siren music of our own ego! The most terrible thing that can happen to any man is to listen to his own voice and think he hears God. The next most terrible thing is to mistake the false voices about him for God's.

Martin Buber calls for the escape from such idolatry by means of a new conscience that summons men "to guard with the innermost power of their souls against the confusion of the relative with the Absolute. . . ." Learn to know and distinguish your own voice so that it does not lead you astray. Listen to all the Elis who may call you until you cannot be mistaken. Most of all, take time to become so familiar with the voice of God through the ages and in our time that you know when to say, "Speak, Lord, for thy servant hears."

+ God's Gift to Me
I Samuel 17:31-40

> Then Saul clothed David with his armor. . . . Then David said to Saul, "I cannot go with these; for I am not used to them."

Saul was reputed to have stood head and shoulders above the average Israelite, and he doubtless had chest and shoulders to match his height. No wonder a teen-age lad like David had trouble with Saul's armor. No one could blame the boy for trying it on. What boy would not want to see if he could wear the king's armor? But David could scarcely walk in such oversized hardware!

Although David was moved by all the notions and dreams of a boy, he still had a strong strain of the practical. He had a job to do; and when he used the weapons to which he was accustomed, the simple sling and the smooth stones from the brook bed, he did the job effectively. The giant Goliath was felled by a common stone cast by a skilled hand from a shepherd's sling.

47

There is always a temptation to wish for the king's armor when a king-size job has to be done. Sometimes the tools to which our hands are accustomed seem strangely crude when we look upon the wonderful equipment God has given to others. There is no reason why we should not make every effort to improve our own abilities toward rendering a more perfect service, but never belittle the gift of God that has become common in your hand.

A rabbinical legend about this same David says that he left behind, at his death, a shepherd's flute carved by his own hand out of a hollow reed. It gave forth the sweetest music in Israel. Someone, however, troubled that so important a memento was so common in appearance, had it decorated with silver and gold. Ever afterward, the little instrument, originally so melodious, produced only a harsh metallic shrillness. God's special gift to you needs only faithful use and true appreciation for its perfecting.

✓ Roots
Matthew 13:18-23

> ". . . he has no root in himself, but endures for a while, and when tribulation or persecution arises on account of the word, immediately he falls away."

We have an advantage over the disciples of Jesus in that we can read the meaning of the parable even before we read the parable. We can recognize the hazards faced by the sower as he sets forth to do his planting.

His greatest problem is really to get the seed into the soil. Some simply falls upon the hard path, so it is easily snatched away. Jesus explains that there are those who never actually grasp the fact that the "word of the kingdom" has any application to them. No wonder the seed does not grow.

Those portrayed by the shallow soil of the rocky ledge do receive the word as their own. The seed quickly sprouts and, all too quickly, wilts. They are excited and enthusiastic about that which is offered to them, but, when they must offer something of themselves, they lose their enthusiasm. They have no root in themselves.

The weedy soil is especially typical of our day when the seeds of many ideas and purposes fall so thickly upon us. What chance does the good growth of the kingdom of God have when we are so busy giving the best nurture of our lives to the crowded weeds of our overgrown "civilization"? Our problem then is not that we have no root in ourselves but that we are "root-bound" with so many roots within us that none has a chance.

We need to cultivate the trodden paths of life until they can nourish good seed once more. Enthusiasms can be deepened until it is possible for seed to find ample rootage. It is important to pull the weeds of life in order that the fullness of life is not wasted in producing the crabgrass of the ages.

OF GOOD AND EVIL

— Making the Best of the Worst
John 9:1-12

"Rabbi, who sinned, this man or his parents, that he was
born blind?"

Why do dread afflictions plague mankind so often without any
apparent reason? This was the source of the question in the
minds of the disciples when they saw the man who had been
born blind.

They assumed that they understood the major portion of
the solution of the problem. They only wanted a little explanation of the details. They were sure that all the evils and
sufferings of life were the result of God's punishment for sin.
The great problem in their thinking lay in the fact that God
could punish the innocent for the sin of the guilty. "Who
sinned," they asked, "this man or his parents?"

Jesus was willing to discuss the puzzling realities of theology
when such discussions could be significant, but he was swift
to turn to the practical when it was needed. It is as if he were
saying, "Let us not waste time discussing the good or evil
done by this man or his parents. The important thing is that
this man's affliction gives us a chance to be used of God in
helping him."

Man has always been troubled by the existence of evil in a
world that is "our Father's world." The searching mind must
always continue to ask the question "Why?" But, while we
are asking our questions, let us not forget that the very imper-
fection of the world gives us the wonderful joy and opportunity to be "workers together with God" in the perfecting

of his purpose. We cannot be overcome by evil or by our wonderment about it. By God's good grace, we must learn to "overcome evil with good."

— Comfort
Job 23:1-10

> "Oh, that I knew where I might find him, that I might come even to his seat!"

The sufferings of Job are proverbial, and the consolations offered by his would-be comforters have become one of the standing jokes of literary history. Job's poor comforters came with undoubtedly good intentions to minister to him in his great need. If they left him feeling worse than he had felt before their comforting, we really cannot be too hard on them. They are distressingly modern in their attitudes.

All that they desired was for their friend to be happy. They wanted a "Hollywood" ending. The total desire of the comforters might be summed up in the single hope that he might have restored to him all that he had lost—health, wealth, and family. What more could one ask?

Job's single desire probed more deeply. Reduced to a simple statement, his prayer might be, "In hardship or blessing, O that I could find God!"

One must never belittle the trials and afflictions of humanity. They are "the dark night of the soul." But, even in darkness, one walks with confidence if he is aware of the Presence of One who knows all the ways. If "he knows the way I take" one can more easily endure the trial and "come forth as gold."

— I Told You So
Jonah 4:1-11

"I pray thee, Lord, is not this what I said? . . . for I knew that thou art a gracious God and merciful, slow to anger, and abounding in steadfast love, and repentest of evil."

"I told you so," said Jonah like a peevish child. "I warned the Ninevites of destruction, and now that they have repented, you have let them off!" Then he went to sulk under his hut of branches overshadowed by his favorite gourd plant. Can you imagine anyone complaining because he knew God to be a God of love?

We, too, have our complaints. Why does God let such things exist? Why does he allow such people to live? We would destroy them, but he would redeem them. Jonah thought more of his gourd plant than he did of a whole city full of people.

Have we been guilty of thinking more of various other material things than we do of people? Why does God not destroy the Russians, for our standard of living is in jeopardy when we waste so much in using their methods to keep them in check? Why does God not take our good advice to overcome the evil that is in the world? So we perpetuate our hates and prejudices, the shortness of our sight and the hysteria of our minds.

God's purpose will be accomplished. When our little gourds have withered into dust, we shall rejoice that he is a "gracious God and merciful, slow to anger, and abounding in steadfast love. . . ."

✛ Fret Not
Psalm 37:1-11

Be still before the Lord, and wait patiently for him;
fret not yourself over him who prospers in his way.

In these first few verses of the thirty-seventh Psalm there is a kind of refrain. Over and over again it sings, "Fret not yourself." When we hear it, we can believe that people have not changed greatly since the day of the psalmist. How easy it is to look around childishly and fretfully fuss and complain over the prosperity of the undeserving! We find ourselves coveting "all this and heaven too."

The psalmist has some good advice for all who are plagued with such fretfulness. "Trust in the Lord, and do good," he says. Fretting shows a lack of such trust, and doing good is a big enough job that it leaves no time for fretting.

He continues, "Commit your way to the Lord; trust in him, and he will act." Your "way" in the psalm deals with the journey of life. To commit your life to God means a sincere enlistment in the greatest cause that can command a man's loyalty. It involves all of one's mind, heart, and will. So much concentration of purpose is necessary that no time is left to pass judgment upon the evil or to explore the reasons for their prosperity. Leave that to God. "He will act."

He concludes his good counsel with, "Be still before the Lord, and wait patiently for him. . . ." How impatient we get with the patience of God! We would have the day of judgment come much more quickly. Seldom do we realize that, in God's sight, every day is a day of reckoning.

This wise psalm reminds us of things we easily forget. God has things in hand—never fret. All the returns are not in—never fret. We do not know all the facts behind the evil of the wicked nor the goodness of the good—never fret. If we can learn to "be still before God," we shall stop our chattering and complaining and fretting.

✝He Cares for You
I Peter 5:1-11

Cast all your anxieties on him, for he cares about you.

No man is exempt from the anxieties of life. Frustration, fear—the possibilities and uncertainties are so many and so varied that they touch every man, regardless of wealth or poverty, health or affliction, keen intellect or dull understanding. Anxiety is part of a great human heritage, a bond that binds all men together. The great difference in men is found in the way in which they handle their anxieties.

One man faces the challenge as if he alone, of all mankind, were the only man afflicted. He feels as if he were singled out for all "the slings and arrows of outraged fortune." He whines in despair, or becomes bitter about everything, because of his misfortune.

Another type of man recognizes that he partakes of common experience when he sticks in "the Slough of Despond" or struggles up "the Hill Difficulty." He may bow his head in passive submission to the inevitable and plod hopelessly onward or calmly wait until all burdens fall and all problems are solved. He sets for us a high example of stoic courage, but life loses zest, and there is no joy in him.

The first Epistle of Peter gives us a clue to another possibility. The long, hard journey of life is not a solitary voyage, nor are we limited only to companions in our misery. A basic significance of Christianity is summed up in the writer's capsule appraisal of God's concern, "for he cares about you." No man is too small nor his problem too limited—"for he cares about you." No man has gone so far beyond redemption—"for he cares about you." No man is too secular, too dense, too unspiritual in outlook. God cares, and scales can fall from human eyes. Then let the Divine Companion of the Way put a shoulder under the load of your anxiety, "for he cares about you!"

✓ God's Fair Play
Matthew 5:43-48

> ". . . for he makes his sun to rise on the evil and on the good, and sends rain on the just and on the unjust."

Is it quite fair for God to allow so many good things to come to evil people? The most difficult lesson of the Christian faith is that which teaches us to return good for evil, and most of us fail in our final examinations. When, very occasionally, we do not fail, we are recognized as "sons of your Father who is in heaven," because, at that moment, there is a strong family resemblance.

God is difficult for us to understand when he does so much good for those whom we regard as wicked. But God is even more difficult for us to understand under exactly opposite circumstances, when he allows what we call evil to fall upon the good. If it is hard for us to see why he should make "his sun to rise on the evil [as well as] on the good," how much more difficult is it for us to grasp the reason why he "sends rain on the just [as well as] on the unjust."

Storms break upon our lives with disastrous circumstances. Affliction, bereavement, catastrophe come often without warning. A good friend, courageously facing a tragic bereavement, writes, "We have not felt punished nor persecuted. We are members of the human race and share its destiny, and God never promised the rain would fall on everyone but us." Is that not the answer? Even God suffered through his Son in entering the human race. Though we cannot answer why, the rain as well as the sun is needed for the nurture of the good life. Let us welcome both as gifts of a loving Father.

✝ Seedtime and Harvest
Matthew 13:1-9

> "Other seeds fell on good soil and brought forth grain, some a hundredfold, some sixty, some thirty."

A bus company in a large city advertised, "We like our business, we meet so many wonderful people." Jesus must have had a very deep conviction that there were many wonderful people in the world. We often become so involved in dealing with the unproductive soil on which the sower scattered his seed that we forget the parable is balanced in the direction of the productive soil.

If some seed fell on the trodden path, some also fell on good soil to bring forth a hundredfold harvest. That which failed to grow on the rocky ledge was overbalanced by that which brought forth sixtyfold. For each seed that was choked out by the weeds, thirty came to fruition in the soil that produced thirtyfold.

Life has its hazards and disappointments that loom large in our sight, but do not let them hide the opportunities and encouragements. It is interesting that Jesus mentioned the productive soil in an order of decreasing return, some a hundredfold, some sixty, some thirty. Certainly he praised God for the extraordinary individual who did more than anyone could dare to expect, but he never forgot the faithful and steadfast producer of the thirtyfold harvest.

We may never be regarded as those disciples of old of whom it was said, "They turned the world upside down," but we can give cause to be remembered among the too often forgotten multitudes who, by faithful effort and steadfast service, keep the world right side up.

— Out of Great Tribulation
Revelation 7:9-17

> "These are they who have come out of great tribulation;
> they have washed their robes and made them white in
> the blood of the Lamb."

How fortunate we are to have suffered no persecution, none of the destruction of war, no hunger, no threat of exile! How fortunate we are! Yet, to find ourselves included with the saints, we must rewrite the book of Revelation. "Who are these, clothed in white robes, and whence have they come?" "These are they who have never suffered for their faith, the lucky ones who were always full when others hungered, who were safe and secure when bombs dropped on other countries, who had more telephones, autos, gadgets, luxuries while others had less clothing, food, education, and the necessities of life." How fortunate we are!

But God could wipe away every smile from our faces! Does God deal so unequally with his children forever? Must we wash our robes (purify our lives) and make them white in the blood of the Lamb (the new way of abundant life won, demonstrated, and made permanent by Jesus Christ)?

Jesus once said, "Greater love hath no man than this, that he lay down his life for his friends." But he was unduly modest. There is a greater love, and God through Jesus demonstrated it. He lay down his life even for those who had no claim upon his friendship. Since then, we cannot pass carelessly by the procession of those who came "out of the great tribulation." We can count ourselves fortunate when we are allowed to be a part of the procession. If they hunger, we hunger with them. Their suffering is pain in our hearts. When they are persecuted and driven forth homeless, our homes are open to them. God is using us to "wipe away every tear from their eyes."

✓The Day of the Lord
Psalm 118:9-29

This is the day which the Lord has made; let us rejoice and be glad in it.

There are tones of rapture in the voice of the psalmist as he sings, "This is the day which the Lord has made." It was a day of glory when Israel had triumphed over her enemies. The psalmist saw things from the point of view of his time, so the victory revealed the firm and loving hand of God.

In a day of rejoicing, a great joy is enriched and sanctified as man becomes aware of the goodness of God. But the Lord has made other days also. Amos, the prophet, warned the comfortable, the indifferent, the hypocritical, the wicked, that a "Day of the Lord" would come when men would be tested in motive, in act, in attitude. Such a day would be one of darkness, not light, for the careless and the sinful.

It was Jesus who gave his disciples the most profound advice about the days that God gives to us with such absolute equality and generosity. Take them one at a time, and trust God through each one. This is what Jesus was saying when he urged no anxiety for tomorrow. Each day has its own problems. (Sufficient unto the day is the evil thereof.) God knows not only all your problems but all their solutions. Trust him to meet your need!

CHRISTIAN VOCATION

✓ The Called Life
Ephesians 4:1-16

. . . lead a life worthy of the calling to which you have
been called.

Being a Christian did not mean simply joining a church to
Paul. To be a Christian was to respond to a call of God that
implied just what Jesus meant to his disciples when he called,
"Follow me." When one responded, he became a "disciple"
or a "learner."

One who is learning may make many mistakes; but, if he
is serious, he never quits. He tries to master the subject in a
way that is worthy of the subject. It was in this way that Paul
challenged his Christian friends to lead lives "worthy of the
calling to which you have been called."

It was entirely human that some would think one aspect
of the Christian life and witness to be more important than
another. But Paul set them right. God has given to us many
various gifts. Each uses his gift to the limit of his ability until
the whole church, the whole Body of Christ, is strengthened.

Paul recognized that the most meaningful *unity* is not *uniformity* but the uniting of a diversity of gifts. Only then do
we begin to understand the meaning of Jesus Christ, who
brought *many* gifts to many people. It is only when people of
diverse talents can bring *varying* gifts to serve *one* great, common purpose that they begin to show signs of what the apostle
calls "mature manhood." Until then, we are indeed "children,
tossed to and fro and carried about with every wind of doctrine."

— Called to Be Saints
Romans 1:1-7

> To all God's beloved in Rome, who are called to be
> saints. . . .

Paul was writing to the Christians of Rome, and he refers to
them as those who are "called to be saints." How the church
has narrowed the idea of sainthood through the ages! "Saint"
has become a title instead of a way of life. It describes those
who have reached a kind of human perfection instead of those
who have committed themselves to the Christian way of life.

There are many imperfect saints. Let us do honor to
"Saint" Paul and "Saint" Mary and "Saint" Francis, but always remember that we too are "called to be saints." The
word properly describes a person set apart for God's purposes
as Paul was set apart for his work of sharing the gospel.

A modern saint uses his best thinking in the service of God,
not in the superficialities and meaningless distractions of our
time. The best energy he has to offer is devoted to doing
God's work, not dissipated in the feverish "pursuit of happiness" or the endless climb to social prestige. His first allot-
ment of time, not the leftovers after all his social engagements
have been fulfilled, is given to the purposes of God. Insofar
as we have answered God's call upon our lives, we are set
apart for the gospel as much in our day as Paul was in his.
Imperfect or not, we are "called to be saints."

— Running Away from God
Jonah 1:1-10

> The men knew that he was fleeing from the presence of
> the Lord, because he had told them.

Jonah tried to run away from God. He even had the audacity

to disagree with God. Jonah did not like Ninevites. Nineveh was the capital of a country that had been a traditional enemy of Israel. Why should God show any concern for them?

The Christian notion of forgiveness and of doing good for one's enemies was long in the future. Whoever wrote the book of Jonah was a person of such deep insight that he began to see into the heart of God centuries before Jesus revealed that heart. But there are Jonahs in our day, centuries after the revelation that Jesus brought. For the racist, it must seem very stupid that God created men of other races as human beings. How strange it is when enemies so often act as if they worshiped the same God that we worship! What a shock it will be to the religious bigot ultimately to discover people of other religious faiths "safe in the arms of Jesus!"

We sometimes act as if we could have done a better job in arranging human life than God did. If we are so dissatisfied that we would walk out on the whole business, there is no place to walk.

> If I take the wings of the morning
> and dwell in the uttermost parts of the sea,
> even there thy . . . right hand shall hold me.

We cannot run away from God or from his unconquerable will. It is better to reach out in our bewilderment to clasp the hand of Divine Wisdom until we find our way.

On the Job Training
Exodus 4:10-17

"Who has made man's mouth? . . . Now therefore go, and I will be with your mouth and teach you what you shall speak."

We are not the first generation to make excuses and to try to rationalize our way out of a challenging job. Moses and many others did it long before. The hardest job that we have to solve is the proper appraisal of our abilities. It would be ridiculous for a crow-voiced, tone-deaf individual to try to sing in the choir or for the color-blind to assume the painting of a mural.

However, none of us is so greatly afflicted that he needs to tur his back upon all assignments. The wonder of the complex life we live is that it provides so many pathways to usefulness. But it is still too easy to turn aside from a useful path if we are not willing to try to be useful. Although the end of the trail may not be in sight, if we have the commitment to start, new signposts appear at each corner to guide us aright.

Moses tried to wriggle out of a great responsibility. Not only would God not allow him to escape but he provided the help and guidance that made it possible for Moses to do an impossible job. God always provides "on the job training," and we learn as we dare to do. Who was more surprised than Moses when he saw the results? What you can do with God's leading will surprise you.

— The Eternal Experiment
John 7:14-24

". . . if any man's will is to do his will, he shall know whether the teaching is from God. . . ."

We live in an age of experimentation. Most of the great discoveries of our time began with an hypothesis that was really a sort of "shot in the dark." Someone willed to accomplish a great purpose, to achieve some important cure, to develop some hitherto undeveloped resource. Usually the start is in shadow, an expression of an unfulfilled hope. It takes courage to aim at a difficult mark.

There can be an evil effect in an age of experiment. Impatient young people experiment with exciting forms of evil. Bored adults try something new to add zest to a life that has lost its flavor. Jesus suggests a kind of difficult experiment.

This is an experimentation in the direction of good and of God.

Often we become aware of a daring good in which we might become involved. We hold off, usually as an excuse, because we cannot be certain that this is the will of God. Why not give it a try? Perform the experiment. If it works, we have discovered a little bit more of the will of God for our lives. If the results are uncertain, we can try again. If we will to do God's will, we shall know.

✓ The Equality of Responsibility
Matthew 25:14-30

". . . you have been faithful over a little, I will set you over much; enter into the joy of your master."

The Declaration of Independence states that all men are created equal, but this equality deals with rights, not native endowments, skills, or physical and intellectual gifts. God intended all of us to have the same rights of "life, liberty, and the pursuit of happiness," but he gave us different materials with which to build our lives, different interests in which we use our liberty, and varying goals of happiness that we pursue.

Another equality is made evident in the New Testament. Even as we are equal in rights, so are we equal in responsibility. Each is responsible for making the most of the varying gifts bestowed upon him by God. The two-talent man is not expected to produce five talents worth of gain, but he is expected to do his best with his two talents. The one-talent man was condemned because he did not respond (accept responsibility) to the opportunity offered in the trust of one talent.

Do not let what you cannot do stand in the way of what you can do. To fulfill our limited responsibilities faithfully prepares us ultimately for a greater responsibility.

— First Love
Revelation 2:1-7

> "But I have this against you, that you have abandoned the love you had at first."

One of the measures of maturity is the ability to see a thing through. It is not too difficult to work up an initial enthusiasm over a new idea. The problem comes when one tries to maintain enthusiasm when the going is hard.

The Christians to whom John was writing at Ephesus had thrilled to the first preaching of the Christian Way. They had responded so enthusiastically that the makers of images of Diana of the Ephesians were afraid that their business would be ruined. That is why Paul and Silas became involved in a riot. The gospel of Jesus Christ opened windows on a whole new way of life, and the people of Ephesus opened their hearts to the new faith.

When John wrote the book of Revelation on his island of exile, the first impact of Christianity upon Ephesus was long ago and far away. Although it could be inconvenient and dangerous to be a Christian, John reprimanded those who had lost their earlier devotion. They had started well, but they were finishing feebly. The new Christian, radiant in his faith, had loved everyone, and his loving concern reached out to the needs of people about him. Now, when being a Christian was no longer new and their faith was being tested, their devotion to the Lord Jesus Christ weakened. Love and concern for the brethren had become feeble.

What a pity it is to lose the "spiritual glow" of the first excitement of the Christian faith! Let us open the windows of our faith, and let the fresh breeze of a new commitment blow through to fan the waning embers of devotion into living flame.

✝ Our Will and His
Matthew 21:28-32

"And he answered, 'I will not'; but afterward he repented and went.

This parable of Jesus is typical of young people in all ages and in all places. The two sons can be found in almost any home where there are growing young people.

A parent directs his child to do a task. Especially in our time when young people are in such complete revolt against their elders, the response "I will not!" can frequently be heard. But the young would-be rebel has within himself a sense of right and wrong. Although he seldom admits it, he is anxious to do what is right. With as much face-saving as possible, it is more than likely he will come around to obedience.

However, there is another type of son. He may not rebel but he will lean on the parent for all that he can get out of him. If an order is given he responds with a quick "I go, sir," but his heart is not in it. At the first opportunity he deserts his post, and the job is left incomplete.

When Jesus told this story, he was not discussing the psychology of youth. He was illustrating man's response to God. How like the rebellious or the spoiled teen-ager we can become! All of us are familiar with the individual who shirks the duties of his religion, because he "was required to do them when he was young." He is the rebel who cannot be told, even by God. He knows what he ought to do even while he rebels, and sometimes he grows up enough to do it.

Many of us are like the second son. We respond "Yes" to God, but our hearts are not in it. We are easily distracted from our basic task. We assume that "God is love," and everything will come out all right.

"Which of the two did the will of his father?"

_ Invitation to Life
Mark 1:14-20

"Follow me and I will make you become fishers of men."

Here was an invitation to one of life's greatest opportunities. Simon and Andrew, James and John, and Zebedee were probably established in a dependable business. In Zimmermann's familiar painting of "Christ and the Fishermen," Zebedee shows the doubt and hesitance of an old man who is not ready to leave everything to go off and follow a wandering teacher. James and John show the enthusiasm of youth facing a new challenge.

In every life there come moments and days of great opportunity. They may bring a call to a new way of life, as did the Master's call to the fishermen of Galilee. They may offer a new phase of service or a new expression of faith that will add color and meaning to an old way of life. When the fishermen decided to follow Christ, they set out under the guidance of a Master who sanctified all that he touched.

Hear his call also and decide to walk the new way in the company of the great Guide. No job is worth doing if it cannot be done joyfully in his presence. No road is worth traveling if it is a road on which one cannot travel with the Master.

— Why?
Exodus 3:1-6

"I will turn aside and see this great sight, why the bush is not burnt."

"Why?" is the everlasting question of religion. When one asks "why?" about anything, he implies that there must be a reasonable explanation. The sum total of the answers to all our why's indicates that we live in a reasonable universe. This can be a discomforting conclusion to reach because it sends us seeking the reason for our own being in such a reasonable universe.

Moses saw a burning bush and asked why. His answer came quickly. God was using the burning bush to convey a message. Judging from Moses' later response, he might have hurried by, now that he had his answer; but God does not work that way. He had a question also! Why was Moses here in the safety and quiet of the desert when God's people were suffering in Egypt?

We have many questions that we ask about God. The answers we receive are the foundation stones of our faith. But beware! As soon as one gets a clear answer about God, he hears a clear question about himself. God is ready to answer your seeking soul, but will you be ready to respond to his questions?

Let Me Do It Myself
Matthew 14:22-33

"O man of little faith, why did you doubt?"

The story of Peter's attempt to walk upon the water is one of the most amazing tales of the New Testament. Some elements in the story are included in Mark and John, but only Matthew deals with this incident. We can rejoice that he included it, for it speaks to our need.

Jesus came through the night to the boat where his storm-tossed disciples were struggling with wind and wave. They were frightened by the strange appearance of Jesus walking on the sea. He calmed their fears, but Peter, with his usual impulsiveness, blurted out, "Lord, if it is really you, use your power, and let me walk upon the waves." The Master reached out his hand and said, "Come." Peter started successfully, but, frightened when he saw the tossing waves about him, he forgot that he was not doing this on his own, and he began to sink. Jesus reached out a hand to save him and uttered his rebuke, "O man of little faith, why did you doubt?"

How often do we ask God to help us with something important and then act as if we were doing it ourselves? An important element of the "good news" that Jesus brought is the assurance that we are not alone. To walk the sea of your life may not be easy, for waves of difficulty and unsolved problems are all about. But you are not walking only in your own strength, O you of little faith!

NOW FAITH IS...

✝ Faith
Hebrews 11:1-7

"Now faith is the assurance of things hoped for, the conviction of things not seen. . . . By faith we understand. . . ."

Faith, to one who has it and knows he has it, is the greatest driving force of the ages. Faith, to one who does not have faith, is simply beyond comprehension. Faith has been regarded as mysterious primarily because too many of those who talk about it have no faith.

The writer of the Epistle to the Hebrews knew what he was talking about. From the limited, popular point of view he got everything backward. Normally, men take the attitude that if one lacks assurance about anything, all that remains possible is to take it on faith. The writer to the Hebrews says clearly, "Faith is the assurance of things hoped for."

The King James version says "substance" instead of "assurance" and is probably closer to the Greek original. "Substance" is that which "stands under" the foundation, let us say, upon which rests all our hope. This is what faith is.

Again, the popular notion is that if one has no real conviction about something, then one must take it on faith. But Christian faith is conviction, a conviction so strong that those eternal things that are unseen are as real as the Rocky Mountains, as dependable as the fixed stars.

Finally, the popular notion suggests, "If you cannot understand, you must resort to faith." Faith becomes a poor substitute for human understanding. Our writer sets things right when he recognizes that it is often "by faith we understand."

We can be very grateful for the five senses by which we are aware of so much that is around us. Because we realize that physical senses are sometimes unreliable, we can be grateful that they do not offer our only clues to reality. For the Christian there is more—the assurance, the conviction, the understanding of faith.

⌐ Beyond the Hills
Psalm 121:1-8

> I will lift up my eyes to the hills.
> From whence does my help come?
> My help comes from the Lord,
> who made heaven and earth.

Hills are a part of the gothic structure of the universe. As the gothic cathedral leads every eye upward with its soaring arches, so the hills lift our eyes above the valleys in which we dwell.

In the public square of the little French town of Chamonix at the foot of Mont Blanc, there is a statue of the first man to have scaled that mountain. He is pictured looking up at that snow-covered peak. If you look carefully, you will discover that the line of his vision, although it follows the steep slope of the mountain, goes far beyond the peak.

The psalmist was inspired by hills as we are, but his inspiration went beyond the hills. Not in the tallest mountain does one find his ultimate "refuge and strength." It is in the Creator of the hills.

This psalm is one of the pilgrim songs of ancient Israel. The journey to Jerusalem must have been tiring and dangerous in those days. One did not travel to the Holy City in a few hours as in a modern automobile. The trip could take many days. When darkness came, the tents were pitched. The pilgrim could look out through the flap in the tent and lift his eyes to the hills beyond. Those were the hills where David's band of outlaws hid in days long gone by. From those hills the guerilla bands of the Maccabees were to come down upon the hapless Greek invaders in days to come. It is even possible that these were the hills down which a good Samaritan would one day travel to find a Jew, beaten and robbed, lying at the wayside.

All this could not be in the pilgrim's mind, but in many periods of Hebrew history he might well have looked upon the hills with fear. But there was something much more important in his thinking. He raised his eyes to the hills with every assurance that above, beyond the hills was God, keeping faithful watch above his own. Who can fear?

— Whom Shall I Fear?
Psalm 27:1-14

> One thing have I asked of the Lord,
>   that will I seek after;
> that I may dwell in the house of the Lord
>   all the days of my life. . . .

Psalm 27 was written by a man in trouble, but he faced that trouble with the courage and faith that made him able to conquer it. I expect that the first words of the psalm were addressed to himself. They were a kind of determined whistling in the dark until the light came. He was timorously saying, "Who's afraid! God is with me!" Then, suddenly, he discovered that God was really there.

This is a psalm of that true faith that is "the assurance of things hoped for, the conviction of things not seen." It has been suggested that it was written by one of the Levites whose whole life was spent in the service of the Temple, for whom "the house of the Lord" was not only a place of worship but a true dwelling place. Although we live in such a different age, the spirit of the psalm has profound implications for us.

The great yearning of the psalmist to "dwell in the house

of the Lord all the days of my life" is but a shadow of the deep human longing to "feel at home" with God at all times and in all places. Under such circumstances, "Though a host encamp against me, my heart shall not fear." It is only as we are convinced that our life and work are a part of the will of God that God becomes our "light and salvation." Then we can rise above all circumstances and live above fear.

✝ All I Need
Psalm 42:1-11

> Why are you cast down, O my soul,
>   and why are you disquieted within me?
> Hope in God. . . .

The psalmist is giving himself a justifiable scolding. Even in the face of circumstances that have produced disheartenment and doubt he knows that the One who is for him is more than all that is against him.

No one really knows the meaning of life without the experience of walking through similar shadows and finding a similar gleam of light. The poet has said:

> O blest is he to whom is given
> The instinct that can tell
> That God is on the field when He
> Is most invisible!

I interviewed a refugee whose story of loss, persecution, and suffering was the epitome of man's inhumanity to man. After summing up his experience, he said, "I have nothing left but God." Then he paused a moment and added, "But that is all I need."

One's sanity is questioned if he talks too much to himself. Yet, in the dark days when we lose sight of the great Reality, we need to take ourselves by the scruff of the neck to give ourselves the kind of scolding that the psalmist knew he needed.

Why are you cast down, O my soul,
  and why are you disquieted within me?
Hope in God; for I shall again praise him,
  my help and my God.

✝ Pillar of Cloud
Exodus 13:17-22

The pillar of cloud by day and the pillar of fire by night
did not depart from before the people.

What a sense of assurance to have a tall pillar of cloud to
indicate the right road! Some scholars have suggested that it
was smoke rising from the volcanic mountain that was sacred
to the worship of the Lord. But it must have been even more
reassuring when the dark night of the desert came down
around them to see, clear through the darkness, the glowing
pillar of fire still marking the way.

The billowing cloud of our confidence in God's leading
shows clearly the road we should take. Then comes the dark,
and we grope to find our way. No man travels always by the
bright light of day.

Through the night of doubt and sorrow,
Onward goes the pilgrim band.

Disturbing questions arise within us, and no answer is to be
found. Afflictions come suddenly, and we can discover no
reason. Loved ones depart, or those whom we have trusted
disappoint. The light goes out in the sky, and we stumble in
the darkness.

This is just the point at which we search for the "pillar of
fire by night," and there, on the dark horizon, we can find it
if we truly seek.

Clear before us through the darkness
Gleams and burns the guiding light;
Brother clasps the hand of brother,
Stepping fearless through the night.

The Unconquerable
Romans 8:28-39

. . . we are more than conquerors through him who loved us.

Life's problems and heartaches do not make it easy to see that "in everything God works for good with those who love him, who are called according to his purpose." Paul had not lived a sheltered existence, exempt from life's hardships, but he was absolutely certain that God's good purpose was steadily working through every circumstance, no matter how unfortunate the situation might seem.

Someone has said, "One man with God is a majority." Paul lived by this faith when he said, "If God is for us, who is against us?" The sense of his question is, "If God is for us, what difference does it make who may be against us?" The hazards were as great then as now—tribulation, distress, persecution, famine, nakedness, peril, or sword. In the face of all these and many more difficulties, Paul knew "in all these things we are more than conquerors through him that loved us."

This is not whistling in the dark. A frightened pilot might well do that to keep his courage up, but the sound of his own whistle does not help much. When he locates the clear shining of a guiding light, he knows he has found real help. Then he can safely navigate the dark seas until he reaches harbor. The unfailing love of God revealed through Jesus Christ our Lord is the clear light for the Christian. That light never fails.

Shelter
Psalm 91:1-16

You will not fear the terror of the night,
nor the arrow that flies by day,
nor the pestilence that stalks in darkness,
nor the destruction that wastes at noonday.

We live in a strange time. We have devised more labor-saving devices than our grandparents could have dreamed of. Yet we are so weary that we cannot sleep at night. We are surrounded by constant attempts to entertain us, to make us laugh. Yet we are not happier than our forebears. We have more means of defense than the most ingenious men of war could have imagined in all the ages past. Yet we are in the grip of an hysterical fear that leads some political leaders to suggest a law to require an atomic shelter in every home.

We need a shelter, but it was built for us before time began. The psalmist realized this when he wrote:

He who dwells in the shelter of the Most High
. . . will say to the Lord, "My refuge and my fortress;
my God, in whom I trust."

The man of faith always lives a life of exciting risk. He is entirely aware that the evil of man is a constant threat to his physical safety. Man can, if he will, use evil to try to counteract the threat, but he only succeeds in increasing the evil. Or he can, at awful risk, live as a man with faith in the ultimate victory of God and his will. Though the complete victory may not be seen in his lifetime, the man of faith lives or dies in the knowledge that he is part of eternal values. Terror, pestilence, destruction may come, but he will not fear. The shelter of the Most High is the greatest shelter of all.

THE CHURCH
SPEAKS TO OUR TIME

✓The Church in Your House
Romans 16:3-5, 25-27

> Greet Prisca and Aquila, my fellow workers in Christ
> Jesus . . . greet also the church in their house.

The first Christian churches could not be identified with a
building. The church then, as now, can only be thought of
properly in terms of people.

Some of the people who were the Christian church in Rome
can be identified by name, for Paul sent his greeting to them
personally. It was their custom to meet in a private home
when they gathered for the fellowship of worship or united
in prayers for their brethren.

We have associated the idea of church so much with the
meetinghouse in which the church gathers that we sometimes
find it difficult to recognize the true meaning of the word.
When Paul greeted the church in the house of Prisca and
Aquila, he probably referred to the group of Christians who
usually met there, but devoted Prisca and courageous Aquila
were also thought of by the Apostle as the "church in their
house."

You and your family are "the church in your house," and
the church that gathers in the meetinghouse on the Lord's
Day has little meaning unless it is composed of the church
from many homes. The Lord's Day meant much to the first
Christians, but "the light of the world" was not just the flicker
on a Sunday altar for them. It was the steady flame of the
devoted spirits who, through all the week, let the light shine
from "the church in their house."

✓ The Measure of Religion
Amos 5:18-24

> But let justice roll down like waters, and righteousness
> like an everflowing stream.

Amos lived in the midst of the most vigorous expression
of organized religion in his day. Services must have been well
attended at the "King's Chapel" in Bethel. Nowhere would
one find feast days and holy seasons celebrated with more
pomp and circumstance. But it was a kind of Sunday-go-to-
meeting religion that did not affect daily living.

It is entirely possible for a man with no religious experience to be honest and just, kind and considerate, faithful and
responsible, but one expects to find such attributes in the life
of a man who has a true religious experience. If they are
lacking, there is reason to question the validity of his religion.

Like Amos, we live in a time and place where the outward
expressions of religious faith are all about us. But homes are
crumbling, morals are lax, dishonesty is regarded as cleverness,
racial and international tensions increase. What is the significance of the apparent vigor of religion? At very least, it is
an awareness of God. But God still says, "I hate, I despise your
feasts, and I take no delight in your solemn assemblies" unless
"justice rolls down like waters, and righteousness like an ever-
flowing stream."

Prepared to Worship
Ecclesiastes 5:1-7

> Guard your steps when you go to the house of God; to
> draw near to listen is better than to offer the sacrifice
> of fools. . . .

The writer of Ecclesiastes had a hard time sensing the reality
of God. Yet the struggles of doubt often reveal the basic

truths of faith. This is obvious in this skeptical writer as it is in other "wrestlers for the Lord" through the ages. The "Preacher" offers sage advice when he says, "To draw near to listen is better than to offer the sacrifice of fools."

Religion, in all its organized forms, falls into two great errors. In the first place, religious people often get the notion that they are doing something for God, while, all along, God is doing something for them. How often have you felt a sense of self-righteous satisfaction when you have given up some planned pleasure to attend worship or to perform some religious duty? We even catch ourselves talking about the "sacrifices" we make for our church or for our faith. Are these "the sacrifices of fools"? It should be our greatest privilege to be aware of God in the fellowship of worship or in our solitude. Our greatest pleasure should lie in the knowledge that God constantly does for us what we cannot do for ourselves in the family of the church or on the lonely frontiers of personal conflict.

In the second place, organized religion tends to settle into forms and rituals, into regulations and requirements that become so important in themselves that we often lose sight of what they are intended to accomplish. It takes constant vigilance on our part that the windows through which we look on God and his purposes do not shine so dazzlingly in our eyes that we see only the windows.

"Draw near to listen" rather than to speak. Be more ready to hear God than to tell him.

⌒ The Fellowship of Saints
Hebrews 11:32-40

> All these, though well attested by their faith, did not receive what was promised, since God had foreseen something better for us, that apart from us they should not be made perfect.

We are one of the links in that great chain of human experience that holds history together. From the Christian point of view this is part of the meaning of the traditional phrase "the Fellowship of Saints." Not only are we properly one with the people of faith throughout the world, but we are also bound to all those who have named the name of Jesus Christ throughout time.

The catalog of the "saints" in the letter to the Hebrews goes far back beyond Christian tradition, although the final summation of the martyred and persecuted could be considered descriptive of the great spirits of Christian history.

Two important facts are evident in the unexpected climax of the eleventh chapter of the Epistle to the Hebrews. First, what an unshakable foundation of triumphant faith has been laid for us through the ages by those who have gone before! Second, what an obligation rests upon us if they who have lived and labored in our behalf "should not be made perfect" except we do our part!

They have run the greatest marathon relay of history. The torch has passed from hand to hand. What if we runners of the present lap were to stumble and fall? We are the present bearers of a glorious responsibility, for "God had foreseen something better for us, that apart from us they should not be made perfect."

✓The Strong and the Weak
Romans 15:1-13

We who are strong ought to bear with the failings of the weak, and not to please ourselves. . . .

There are two basic and diametrically opposed philosophies of life. One of them might be phrased in the trite statement, "Might is right." It is all right to do anything you are strong enough to get away with. Do not be hindered in your desires or ambitions because there are weaklings around you. This was the philosophy of Adolf Hitler and of other dictators.

They have often implemented this belief to the extent of liquidating the afflicted, who in their weakness got in the way of the strong.

A different philosophy is contained in the Christian attitude toward life. Strength is a blessing, but it also implies a responsibility. The strong need to take the weak into account and set their pace accordingly.

Behind all this is a profound recognition that even the strong have their weaknesses. The strong man who helps the physically weak along the way may be the spiritual weakling who needs his weak brother's strength when he faces a situation not to be solved by physical power. Beyond such comparisons is the frank Christian recognition that the greatest human power, physical, intellectual, or spiritual, is but weakness beside the limitless resources of the Almighty.

✔ To Whom Do We Belong?
Romans 14:1-12

> None of us lives to himself, and none of us dies to himself. If we live, we live to the Lord, and if we die, we die to the Lord; so then, whether we live or whether we die, we are the Lord's.

The most important fact of life or death for Paul was that we belong to God and to each other because of our relationship to God. It is tragic that the practice of calling each other "brother" and "sister" within the Christian fellowship became so superficial that it fell into disuse. If such a form of address could be kept on the proper level, it would constantly remind us of the close relationship of the family of the Christian faith. One is our Father, so we are all brothers!

It is disturbing to discover how many petty details have entered into the divisions of the church. We should find foundations for unity in our basic faith in God, in our concept of the significance of Jesus Christ, and in the evidences of the working of the Holy Spirit in the lives of men bearing different signs and symbols. But how critical we are of petty details! It is too easy for us to hold lightly what may be of supreme importance to our brother.

We need Paul's admonition that the important issues of life and death are beyond our childish control. We belong to God! When we face the ultimate challenges of life, we know that we are but children, peevish and quarrelsome. Our Lord is all.

Can we consider our differing brethren with humility? They, too, belong to God. The family of God becomes united, not by our stubborn insistence upon our way, but by our recognition that we are all children of one Father and our determined effort to understand and to love our brothers.

† On Being Different
Romans 12:1-8

> Do not be conformed to this world but be transformed by the renewal of your mind, that you may prove what is the will of God, what is good and acceptable and perfect.

There are two ways to deal with the pagan world in which we live. On the one hand, we can act and think and be as nearly like everyone else as possible. So long as we do not think too deeply, we can be comfortable and at ease, and no one will feel under any compulsion to change.

On the other hand, we can move in a different direction in spite of the crowd and try to change things for the better. Such action or attitude will not increase our popularity. Mary Antin in *The Promised Land* said, "So do we often build our world on an error, and cry out that the universe is falling to pieces, if any one but lift a finger to replace the error by truth." It takes courage to be different in a world that idolizes conformity.

Paul asks Christians to be different, to "be transformed by the renewal of your mind." There is really no other way to be different, for, if one's mind is not truly renewed, there is no real transformation. A change of clothes, or friends, or habits has no significance unless it is indicative of an honest inward change of spirit, or attitude, or thought.

The conversion of Paul on the road to Damascus came when he began to think differently. Francis of Assissi cast aside his extravagant and frivolous habits and started the long road to sainthood when he began to think differently. Wilfred Grenfell, led to think differently by hearing Moody in London, became a man transformed. "Do not be conformed . . . but be transformed by the renewal of your mind. . . ." There is a "will of God" for you.

⊕ Fences and Neighbors
Luke 10:25-37

He, desiring to justify himself, said to Jesus, "And who is my neighbor?"

Robert Frost quoted an old New England proverb in one of his poems when he said, "Good fences make good neighbors." Like so many traditional sayings, this one expresses a dangerous half truth, as Frost clearly understood. I suppose it means that, if we keep our distance from those about us, we shall not become needlessly involved in unneighborly discord and disagreement.

The proverb has no relationship to Jesus' timeless story about the neighborliness of the good Samaritan. That was not the good neighborliness of the good fences. From one point of view, both priest and Levite would fit the definition of the proverb. They quickly built fences to separate them from the wounded man. What those fences were we can only guess. They could have been rationalizations: "The poor chap is too far gone for anyone to help," or "What little I could do would not be of any value." They could have been the excuses that the pressure of an important appointment left no time to turn aside, or that no useful purpose would be served because perhaps the robbers might return to take advantage of a second victim.

The Good Samaritan wrecked all the fences. The prejudice that separated him from the Jew lost its importance. The journey on which he was traveling lost its meaning. The limitations of his resources had no significance. *A man needed help!* Who was the good neighbor, the man with fences or the one with none?

⌒ Talk and Power
I Corinthians 4:14-21

> The kingdom of God does not consist in talk but in power.

"The kingdom of God" is one of those exciting phrases that has thrilled thinking Christians for twenty centuries. They have defined it in various ways, but it still means that God is King. To know that God, in his power and wisdom, rules now and shall rule over the faulty and sinful lives of men brings hope and peace when one is in despair because of present problems.

Paul, in this passage, is not thinking of that far-off day when man's striving and failing shall cease and the will of God be acknowledged universally. Instead, he is speaking of that ever present kingdom of God that comes into being whenever an individual accepts the rule of God in himself. Such acceptance is more than a creed or the joining of a church, although both can be included. "The kingdom of God does not consist in talk," or, as Jesus said, "Not everyone saying 'Lord, Lord,' shall enter into the kingdom."

Instead, the kingdom consists in power. It is as if a potent engine were suddenly connected with a limitless dynamo. Its great wheels and pinions, which have stood idle for so long, begin to move with power and purpose. That is what happens to our little lives when we enthrone God as King and submit fully to his will.

⸺The Chain Reaction
Romans 10:5-17

> How are men to call upon him in whom they have not believed? And how are they to believe in him of whom they have never heard? . . . And how can men preach unless they are sent?

When the atomic bomb was developed, we became aware of the possibilities of a chain reaction. Atomic experimentation could be conducted under sufficient controls as to do no harm, if the experiment were limited. However, a point could be reached when one action set off another until the awful destruction of the atomic bomb was achieved.

This *destructive* reaction is a late and horrifying development in human thought. Paul was aware of the world-changing possibilities of a gloriously *constructive* chain reaction.

Salvation, or spiritual health in man, is realizable only when man enters into those right relationships with God which were made possible by Jesus Christ. How many men live an unhealthy life of the spirit because they are not aware of the meaning of Christian faith! It is the Christian's task to communicate the joy and peace and endless potentialities of the Christian Way so that the power of the Way is made evident and attractive to those who do not know it. Then, by the contagion of a living faith, a chain reaction is set off that is beyond all human prediction.

It was such witnessing and such reaction that won men to the Christian faith through the centuries and opened for them the way to abundant life.

Hearing and Doing
Romans 2:12-24

> For it is not the hearers of the law who are righteous
> before God, but the doers of the law who will be justified.

The law of the ancient Jews was so well-founded upon reason
and common sense that it is mainly acceptable to all reasonable people. But the Jewish people had to deal with the problem that plagues all organized religion. Regulation, rite, and
symbol are useful to put into concrete form the spiritual ideals
and purposes that guide our lives. However, we must always
be on guard lest the form become more important than the
spiritual truth it is intended to express.

Paul had difficulty with those who revered the Law, who
could quote the appropriate Scripture, who fulfilled all the
proper forms but lacked sympathy, consideration, and respect
for men of other backgrounds. Paul acknowledged his indebt-
edness to both Jew and Gentile. If a man who was not familiar
with the Law lived and acted according to its finest precepts,
Paul knew that he was acceptable to God. If a man knew
intimately all the teachings of the Jewish faith and could
quote the Law verbatim but lived and acted as if he had
never heard of it, Paul knew he was unacceptable.

Paul could have quoted the Master's word, "Not every
one who says to me, 'Lord, Lord,' shall enter the kingdom of
heaven, but he who does the will of my father. . . ."

The Defeat of Evil
Romans 12:9-21

> Do not be overcome by evil, but overcome evil with good.

We assume too easily that the Christian teaching of returning
good for evil is a fine ideal but a very impractical procedure.

85

The fact of the matter is that human experience demonstrates that the spirit of retaliation leads only to an increase of evil.

Not much intelligence or any spiritual insight is required to fashion a club or gun, or even an atomic device to beat our enemy into submission. Such victory gives us only one guarantee: In the course of time, our beaten enemy or some other enemy can create something even more effective to put us in our place.

Evil is not destroyed by evil. The contagion of evil is more insidious than that of the most contagious disease known. However difficult it may be, the only way in which evil can ever be effectively overcome is by good. If we can only repay curse with curse, we have not only failed to destroy evil, but evil has destroyed our good. If Jesus of Nazareth had damned his executioners, no Christian faith would now exist. Evil would have triumphed completely. Because he prayed honestly for their forgiveness, good overcame evil; and the faith of Christ continues.

Evil men continue their evil ways through the ages. Where any man refuses to reply to evil with evil, at that point he has overcome evil with good. It is never easy, but there is no other way.

_True Worship
Isaiah 6:1-6

> . . . I saw the Lord sitting upon a throne, high and lifted up; and his train filled the temple.

A national catastrophe, the death of a good and great king, sent Isaiah to the Temple. When a man upon whom one has depended is swept aside, and the future is in jeopardy, it is natural for a man of insight to seek God.

In such a situation Isaiah had a vision that changed his life. He saw the Lord. But it is dangerous to be so clearly aware of God. In such a presence man becomes more deeply conscious of his own limitation than at any other time. In the presence of the glory of God, how inglorious we all become! It would indeed be a calloused individual who would not bow in despair to recognize, "I am lost; for I am a man of unclean lips, and I dwell in the midst of a people of unclean lips. . . ."

A true experience of meaningful worship must include such careful self-appraisal. But worship is actual encounter with God, and the sincerely humble man is not left in his despair. The coals from the altar of his worship touch his lips with cleansing power, and he is ready for a new start.

All the false concepts of life are purged away, and a new call is heard. Whatever the task may be that brings a new significance to life, it becomes a joyful challenge. The Infinite calls to the finite creature, "Whom shall I send, and who will go for us?" Then comes the climax of the complete act of worship. It is the moment of commitment expressed by the prophet in his ready response, "Here am I! Send me." So do we truly worship.

✓ Aware of God
Genesis 28:10-17

"Surely the Lord is in this place; and I did not know it."

If we read the story of Jacob against the Christian tradition in which we have been reared, we shall find much to criticize. Jacob secured his father's blessing by a trick; he took advantage of the affliction of age; he cheated his brother out of what was properly his.

The familiar story of Jacob's ladder is a part of the record of his flight from the possible revenge of his offended brother. When Jacob lay down that night to sleep beneath the stars on some ancient desert, he had no notion of anything other than a safe and comfortable campground. But in his dream the heavens opened at that spot, and his magnificent vision and the voice of God came through. No wonder that spot became for him "Bethel," the "House of God," and the "gate of heaven."

Yet, heaven has many gates, and the children of God cannot find a place to lay their heads that is not the house of God. Lie down in peace where you are. The shining vision may not readily come or the clear call of God be easily heard, but the gleaming ladder is close beside you, though you see it not. The messengers of God are continually ascending and descending; and, at some open gate where you least expect it, one day the Voice will be heard.

The Joy of Religion
Psalm 100:1-5

Make a joyful noise to the Lord, all the lands! Serve the Lord with gladness! Come into his presence with singing!

Robert Louis Stevenson once said,

The world is so full of a number of things,

I'm sure we should all be as happy as kings.

Certainly there is so much about us to make us happy that we have little excuse for unhappiness.

It may be that Stevenson has given us a clue to the mystery of man's unhappiness. For too many of us the clue lies in the "number of things" that are ours. Happiness, at its best, is based upon relationships and not upon possessions.

The psalmist calls all men to express their joy and gladness because "the Lord is God! It is he that made us, and we are his!" Our sense of relationship with God makes us feel "at home" in the universe, and only when we feel "at home" are we happy. The unrest of our time and of all time comes when man feels orphaned and alone, a misfit in a world from which he cannot escape.

If you have found the joy of being children of a heavenly

Father rather than pawns of an unknown and absolute Power, rejoice, and let your joy be known. "Make a joyful noise. . . . Serve . . . with gladness! Come . . . with singing! . . . Enter his gates with thanksgiving, and . . . praise! . . . bless his name! For the Lord is good"; and you belong to him, and he belongs to you. When we know this, we cannot be less happy than kings.

✓ Remember the Sabbath Day
Matthew 12:1-8

"If you had known what this means, 'I desire mercy, and not sacrifice,' you would not have condemned the guiltless."

What is our obligation as Christians toward the faithful observance of a sabbath day? First, we must recognize its significance. The Pharisees of Jesus' day had reduced it to a form prescribed by ecclesiastical regulation. They had missed the fact that the sabbath must be a part of one's living experience if it is to have any meaning at all.

The keeping of the sabbath was intended as a constantly recurring tap on the shoulder to remind men of God. In all the rush of daily work with all the necessity of making a living, they needed, as we do, to take time to realize that they were not alone. God is also "working his purpose out." He is concerned with us, and we need to be concerned with him.

In the second place, the keeping of the sabbath is not just a careless tip of the hat to God, after which we hurry on to do whatever we please. It is a time of waiting until the daily distractions roll aside enough to let in a complete awareness of God and of our part in his purpose. If our part is simply the fulfillment of a sacred ritual, the Pharisees were right. Not even human need should interfere. If our part is to seek out God's will and to let it permeate all of life, Jesus was right, and one should do good on the sabbath and on all other days.

89

The sabbath is never isolated. It is not a "day" like Saturday, Sunday, Wednesday, or any other. It is a spirit of awareness. What you are on the sabbath, you are on every other day. What you are on every day, you are on the sabbath, whatever your formal observance. Not ritualistic sacrifice but a spirit of mercy is demanded.

—The New Life
Romans 6:1-11

> We were buried therefore with him by baptism into death, so that as Christ was raised from the dead by the glory of the Father, we too might walk in newness of life.

When the page of one's life is smudged and marred with errors, it is wonderful to turn over a new leaf and to start all over again. The Christian faith makes such a new start possible.

For Paul the difference between the old, stumbling way of irresponsible self-seeking and self-exalting was as different from the new way of Christian commitment as was night from day. A sincere commitment to the will of God brings confidence and assurance, but it also brings the challenge and opportunity of a life full of new meaning and significance. Christian baptism is the symbol of such a commitment.

Jesus' baptism came at that point in his life when he stood revealed before the world that all might know whose side he was on. His formerly quiet and unassuming life was now over. Baptism for the Christian means death to his old and limited life, and a new life as he steps out along a new way. The Christian walks with determination in the direction of God's purpose; and, as he walks, the purpose is more clearly revealed.

OUR TIME
SPEAKS TO THE CHURCH

✝ Ends and Means
Matthew 10:16-23

"Behold, I send you out as sheep in the midst of wolves;
so be wise as serpents and innocent as doves."

We are often tempted to use the devices of the wicked to accomplish the purposes of the good. It never works. Innocent sheep have a hard time in a forest full of wolves.

Yet, goodness needs to be as wise as evil. T. R. Glover, in *The Jesus of History,* indicated that one of the factors by which the Christians of the first century survived and triumphed over their Roman persecutors was that they "outthought" the pagan world in which they lived.

It is tragic in our time that so much thought and ability and God-given talent is wasted upon nonentities. An artist worthy of a better purpose labors to produce a picture that will sell cigarettes or soap flakes. A writer succumbs to the urge of the "best seller" and prostitutes his art to appeal to the lowest instincts of the reading public. Even the church, too, often leaves man as he is for the sake of full pews, instead of helping man become what God intended him to be for the sake of a changed world.

I am not certain how wise serpents may be, but the burden of Jesus' striking illustration is clear. He never belittled the power of evil. We are to use all the wisdom, skill, and artistry that evil uses, but we do it with motivations of love, goodness and godliness that are the basic drives of the Christian life. This is not justifying bad means by worthy ends. Unfortunately, evil is most successful in using good means towards unworthy ends. We need to outthink the pagan world of which we are a part.

✓ Involved
Acts 16:35-40

> "They have beaten us publicly, uncondemned, men who are Roman citizens, and have thrown us into prison; and do they now cast us out secretly?"

Paul had the courage of his convictions. He had been jailed without justice because of his concern for a fellow human being. He had helped a girl who, in our time, would have been considered mentally ill. Her owners brought charges against Paul when they "saw that their hope of gain was gone." What will men do in the name of profit!

One thing can be certain. Paul and Silas had no regrets. A convinced man is free to act upon the demands of his conscience when he is willing to take the consequences of his action. Those consequences are often unpleasant whether in Paul's time or in ours. To face them courageously is the evidence that the act of conscience is not a fad, a publicity stunt, or an attempt to escape responsibility.

One feels almost sorry for the police officials involved in Paul's case. Established, unadjustable authorities never know what to do with a man directed by a good conscience. The criminal they can manage, but the man who is in trouble for a good cause or for his involvement in a worthy but unpopular act is a real problem. Inevitably they have some sympathy with him or some twinge of conscience as they deal with him. Unavoidably they are entangled in the mesh of established law, the complaints of "good citizens," the problem of protecting property or status quo institutions. They try to extricate themselves quietly. Paul, very properly, would not let them. "They condemned us publicly, making us seem evil," he said. "Let them release us publicly and reveal our good."

⅄ The Impossible Possibility
Isaiah 11:1-9

> The wolf shall dwell with the lamb . . .
>   and the calf and the lion and the fatling together,
> and a little child shall lead them.

This is one of the passages of the Old Testament that has sometimes been interpreted as foretelling the effect of the coming of Christ. At any rate, it shows what the prophet believed possible when the spirit of the Lord rests upon a national leader. Under such an influence, the leader possesses "wisdom and understanding," wise counsel, and the power to carry it out in the "knowledge and the fear of the Lord." All the old enmities disappear when the Spirit of the Lord is the accepted guide. The prophet illustrates his point by portraying a kind of blissful world where wolves and lambs, calves and lions can dwell together, and little children need have no fear.

Do we dare to anticipate the kind of world where children can live and grow to maturity without fear or danger? In the old city of Dinkelsbuhl in Bavaria an interesting children's pageant is held every year. It commemorates the time when the armies of Gustavus Adolphus invaded Germany and laid siege to the city. When its inhabitants were reduced almost to starvation, a procession of children was sent forth from the gates to plead for mercy. Hardened soldiers remembered their own little ones at home and were deeply touched. They yielded to the plea of the children, and the city was spared.

It is a hard heart that can feel no concern for the innocent. The Master held a little child on his knee to say, "For to such belongs the kingdom of heaven." The inherited enmities of the ages are not worth the price we pay for them. Do we dare to pay the cost of a world where little ones need fear no harm?

> Though the fig tree do not blossom,
>   nor fruit be on the vines,
> the produce of the olive fail
>   and the fields yield no food,
> the flock be cut off from the fold
>   and there be no herd in the stalls,
> yet I will rejoice in the Lord. . . .

Character is not smoothed into shape by the easy things of life; it is cut and carved by the difficult experiences. The stuff of which a man is made is not so much revealed when "the sun shines bright on my old Kentucky home" as it was "when Israel was in Egypt's land."

The prophecy of Habakkuk comes from troublous times. Violence, corruption, and vice were all about him. His message is full of "woes," so replete with man's inhumanity to man that it is not often read. We have enough of our own troubles to face. Yet, this little treatise finishes on a note of faith and courage that needs to be sounded in all troublous times, including our own.

It is not difficult to express gratitude to God when one is overwhelmed with good things. We are so richly blessed that our surplus and affluence have become a source of embarrassment to us. Materially, our standard of living is higher than that of any people on the globe. We have also entered the era of full churches. The rolls of our religious bodies include a large proportion of the total population of our country. We may well hope that this is some small indication of our awareness of the grace and goodness that God has bestowed upon us.

But suppose an awful change came that made us the refugees instead of the benefactors to refugees? Suppose the crops should fail, "the fields yield no food," our cattle and wealth be lost. Could we still, with the ancient prophet, "rejoice in the Lord"?

✓ Nest in the Stars
Obadiah 1:4

> Though you soar aloft like the eagle,
> though your nest is set among the stars,
> thence I will bring you down,
>> says the Lord.

Man's greatest sin is to assume the prerogatives of God. The single chapter of the book of Obadiah is a "hate song" condemning a nation that tried to play God.

The ancient city of Petra, built in the cleft of the rock on a crag in Edom, might well have been regarded as an "eagle's nest," impregnable, able to defend itself against any enemy. But powerful Petra is now but an imposing ruin, lost in the hills above the Arabah, visited by archeologists and antiquarians. It was the symbol of a nation that cared nothing for her neighbors. Edom stood aloof when her neighbor nation suffered; she gloated over disaster. Edom acted as if she could be independent in a world where no one stands alone. She soared aloft "like the eagle," her nest "set among the stars," but God brought her down, and she is no more.

History is the record of "greatest" nations who, in their national pride, forgot the interdependence of men and became only a page in the record.

There is another implication in the old prophecy of Obadiah. No nation can stand aloof when men suffer, but neither can a nation stand in judgment upon its neighbor nations. All men and nations stand only before the bar of God. Edom deserved her condemnation, but "hate songs" and pronouncements of judgment never redeem either those who utter them or those against whom they are spoken. Today Edom is an ancient memory, but her accusers also failed to heed the lesson of history and experienced devastation. No man and no nation can live without earnest regard for all others—

> though your nest is set among the stars,
> thence I will bring you down,
>> says the Lord.

⊕ Indestructible Truth
Jeremiah 36:20-28

> As Jehudi read three or four columns, the king would
> cut them off with a penknife and throw them into the
> fire in the brazier. . . .

You cannot destroy the truth by burning the paper upon
which it is written! The books of Martin Luther were publicly burned in the shadow of the old cathedral in the ancient
city of Worms, but the truth that they proclaimed became the
foundation of a new attitude toward faith and a new manner
of Christian living.

Jehoiakim, the king, was troubled by the written message
of Jeremiah, the prophet. If the prophet's message were true,
he must turn from his evil way and lead his nation in a new
direction. He burned the message bit by bit, but he discovered
later that the message and the will of God could not be
changed as the parchment was reduced to ashes.

Book-burning is not popular in our time. We have many
other means of censorship, but none of them is really new.
We ridicule the individual who dares to speak an unpopular
truth, but truth goes on. We condemn his character or accuse
him of subversion, but the truth remains unchanged. We do
not burn the Bible but put it in a place of honor where it is
not touched. Even though it remains unread, its truth is timeless. We shout our slogans, laugh the empty laughter of our
inane pleasure, whirl busily about in our endless activity, all
that we may not have to stop to hear the truth that is the only
sure foundation for our lives. The still, small voice of truth
continues to speak quietly through the din. Nothing destroys
the truth. Seek it above all else!

✝ It Is My Fault
Jonah 1:11-17

"Take me up and throw me into the sea; then the sea will quiet down for you; for I know it is because of me that this great tempest has come upon you."

The little book that bears the name of Jonah does not show the prophet in a very favorable light. But there is one moment of glory for him in it. Men have been so concerned with the dramatic details of his being swallowed by a "whale" that the important elements of the story have been lost.

Jonah was placed in the jeopardy of being swallowed by the great fish because he offered himself to be sacrified to save the lives of the other people aboard the ship. It is even more astonishing that he should do this in behalf of a crew who were obviously foreigners in his sight.

The whole problem of the book of Jonah arises because the prophet refused to preach the word of the Lord to foreigners. He felt that it should be shared only by the people of his own nation, Israel. Non-Israelites were beyond the pale, unworthy of consideration. Then his point of view was suddenly changed! These foreigners of the crew were a strangely considerate lot. They hesitated to throw him overboard. They sought in vain for a way to save him. Maybe Jonah was willing to face death in their behalf because, for the first time in his life the foreigner became a living, sharing, understanding, close-at-hand person and not a distant, incomprehensible, impersonal generalization of everything questionable. People, when we know them face to face, are not symbols of racial, national, and ideological misfits, but persons like ourselves.

On Keeping a Bad Promise
Judges 11:2-36

"... you have become the cause of great trouble to me; for I have opened my mouth to the Lord, and I cannot take back my vow."

It is important to be faithful in keeping a good promise when it is made, but it is equally important to have the courage to refuse to keep a bad promise made without proper consideration.

Jephthah would not have understood such a statement, for he lived in a day when a vow was inviolable, whether it was made with careful thought and purpose or carelessly made in a moment of ambition for victory or fear of defeat. God does not change through the ages. Certainly he did not desire human sacrifice then any more than he does now. Jephthah had made a bad promise and lacked the courage to admit it.

A little fellow was reprimanded for helping to cheat in an examination. "But I had promised to help my friend in arithmetic," he protested. "I didn't think he meant that way, but I could not go back on my promise."

The problem of promising begins long before the promise is made. Life needs firm foundations of insight, morality, and integrity. Promises have meaning only when they are built on that kind of foundation. Even then, they can mean something only when they come not out of impulse but out of careful thought and true consideration. Let your promise be a good one when it is made. If by deliberate twist or by quirk of chance the fulfillment of a promise violates the moral premises of life, have the courage to admit a mistake and to erase your promise.

The Conquest of Prejudice
Acts 10:34-43

"... God shows no partiality, but in every nation anyone who fears him and does what is right is acceptable to him."

Many of the early Christians who had come from good Jewish ancestry were amazed when the Holy Spirit came even upon Gentiles. The prejudice of many generations was hard to root out. It is always disturbing to discover how many conflicts and injustices are kept alive out of sheer prejudice.

Most prejudice has a basic *excuse* for being, but it lacks a *reason*. Someone has said, "Prejudice is being down on what you are not up on." It took a heavenly vision to open the eyes of Peter to see that God shows no partiality. Paul reminded the Athenians later that God "made from one every nation of men to live on all the face of the earth." Man, whose prejudice is based on racial and national grudges, acts only in accordance with his human failing, not in the light of God's purpose. Men have tried to rationalize their hatreds for generations, but the fact still remains that God created all men; and at each succeeding stage of his creation he found his work good. Peace can dawn on earth when we find the goodness that he created.

Civil Disobedience
Daniel 6:6-13

... he got down upon his knees three times a day and prayed and gave thanks before his God, as he had done previously.

Daniel believed in what Henry David Thoreau called "the duty of civil disobedience." In every time and in every nation bad laws have been made as well as good, and wrong decisions reached as well as right. What can we do in the face of a legal requirement that we regard as completely wrong?

Patience must be part of the answer, but not all. Jesus told his disciples to pay the tax required by the oppressive Roman government, and Paul urged obedience to the "powers that be." Yet, Jesus preferred a felon's death in dedication to the purpose of his life rather than the security of a life of compromise. And Paul fell constantly athwart the "powers that be" rather than yield the freedom of his preaching.

One must be patient with the slow plodding of blind and careless leadership unless the point is reached that violates the truth as God has revealed the truth, and right, as God enlightens us to see the right. Then we take our stand with full knowledge of the risks involved, for "so persecuted they the prophets which were before you."

History is full of the glory of Stephen, John Huss, Elizabeth Fry, John Bunyan, and all those others who dared to stand for the truth and feared not the consequences. When a cause means so much to you that you are willing to pay for it the price of ridicule and suffering, yield not an inch. It is the truth and righteousness for you.

✓ Another Chance
Jonah 2:10—3:10

> Then the word of the Lord came to Jonah the second time, saying, "Arise, go to Nineveh, that great city, and proclaim to it the message that I tell you."

Even though Jonah did not deserve it, God gave him a second chance. His story is told so vividly that his spiritual failure is clearly evident. Jonah is not telling his own story, or there might be more of rationalization or self-justification in it. Instead, we see the clear portrait of a narrow-minded man, prejudiced against his fellowmen, stubborn in demanding his own way, sulking like a spoiled child when God did not yield to his selfishness. But God still gave him a second chance! While Jonah's uncomplimentary biography is before us, we should do a little work on our autobiography.

How open-minded are we when someone wants something good for those whom we dislike? Are we free from the kind of prejudice that Jonah felt against the Ninevites? Nineveh is safely far away and long ago, but what of the barriers of race or creed or nation we have built? When it becomes obvious that God's way is not our way, are we free from stubbornness and childish sulking? Yet, God gives to us also a second chance.

What joy could have been Jonah's in the success of his preaching! The hated Ninevites might well have become his most grateful and devoted friends. Is there a neglected path ahead that you have avoided by which God could lead you into a new and wonderful opportunity?

⊕ The Cure of Laziness
Proverbs 6:6-11

> Go to the ant, O sluggard;
> consider her ways and be wise.

"Busy as a bee" is the way we put it. The wise man of the book of Proverbs would have said "busy as an ant" to describe someone who was industrious. Whichever way it is expressed, it describes a healthy way of life. Simple laziness has been one of the perennial enemies of mankind.

Our own laziness can be concealed easily by every sort of rationalization. The writer of Proverbs describes this in the twenty-sixth chapter as the sluggard cries, "There is a lion in the streets!" Anything will suffice to postpone what needs to be done.

The ant, in contrast, labors on with great diligence with no necessity for anyone to drive him to his task. Sloth, or laziness, was listed with the seven deadly sins of the Middle

Ages. I expect that it was recognized as the seed from which grows a tragic harvest. It postpones and procrastinates until the precious gift of time is gone and it is too late to accomplish the needed task. It places an unfair burden upon the diligent as they faithfully shoulder their responsibilities. It wastes the skills and talents bestowed by God upon all his children. It disappoints the expectations of those who love us. It misses the opportunity and basic purpose of men to be fellow workers together with the creating God.

But laziness is curable! A bit of human determination, a sense of dedication to something bigger than oneself, a taste of the satisfaction of achievement, an awareness of fellowship with the workers of the earth—all these call irresistibly, "Awake, thou that sleepest!"

_ The Act of Remembering
Lamentations 1:1-7

> Jerusalem remembers
> in the days of her affliction and bitterness
> all the precious things
> that were hers from days of old.

Memories can be a blessing or a curse. The good gift of memory makes possible all the benefits of learning. "The burnt child dreads the fire" only because of the miracle of memory. If he could not recall the painful results of his previous experience, he would burn himself again and again. Memory can fill lonely moments with the joys of the past, and we can look upon familiar faces once more.

But memory can also be an escape from the responsibilities of the present and the future. How many people use the time that might be devoted to making good new days for only remembering the good old days! In modern Jerusalem there remains that little corner of antiquity that is called the "wailing wall." It is reputed to be a portion of what once was the magnificent temple built by Herod on the ancient site of Solomon's Temple. At certain seasons of the year devout Jews used to gather to chant the mournful passages of the book of Lamentations, remembering the glory that was once Israel. Not too many miles away is the remarkable modern city of Tel Aviv, the beating heart of the new Israel. It is an "alabaster city," shining with modern houses, public edifices, and great universities. It was not produced by wailing! The surrounding desert blossoms as a rose, not because of lamentation but by hard and grueling effort.

Let us not cast aside the precious treasure of our memories. Even the memory of anguish has its gift to give. But make that precious memory the seed of the future, so what God has taught us will blossom in faith and fulfillment.

STEWARDS OF AFFLUENCE

✝ Little Lives
Luke 19:1-10

And he sought to see who Jesus was, but could not, on account of the crowd, because he was small of stature.

Zacchaeus was a small man in more ways than one. The fact that he was "a chief tax collector, and rich," did not even begin to make him great. There are many small men in great positions, but there are also a number of great men in small positions.

Zacchaeus shared in the perennial unpopularity of the tax collector. Apparently, from his own admission of fraud, he deserved such a judgment. But something happened to make him great! It takes a great man to admit that he is wrong. And it takes a great man to make restitution. Furthermore, it takes a great man to share his wealth in accordance with the principles of Christian stewardship.

Ernest Hemingway once talked with a newspaper reporter about courage, saying, "There are many kinds. There is the courage of the hunter stalking his prey, of a soldier in battle, and of an old man about to die. But the very greatest kind is around us every day. It is the courage of a man who lives a small life well."

Zacchaeus had lived an important life poorly. We hear nothing further of him in the New Testament beyond this account. In it he begins to live a small life well. Each of us needs the courage of confession, the will to share, the challenge of a high call, and the daring to live our small lives well.

Gift and Giver
Mark 12:41-44

"Truly, I say to you, this poor widow has put in more than all those who are contributing to the treasury."

The value of one's giving lies not in the measure of the gift but in how much one withholds. True it is that the multimillionaire who gives a fortune accomplishes more for the world than the poor man who gives ten dollars out of his poverty. But what does it do for the giver? It can mean the same for both, but usually it does not.

In a world like ours the wealthy are hounded for gifts until the joy of giving is often lost. One feels pressured into the support of countless causes about which one really has little interest. If a gift, large or small, can be given with joy and enthusiasm, not from the necessity of matching competition, maintaining prestige, or escaping taxes, it becomes a part of the growth of one's spirit. Life takes on new meaning, and the enervating boredom of our time is defeated.

Give the great gift if you can afford it, but give it in a great way, not of necessity. If, however, you must be listed among the small givers because of the limitation of your means, do not lose the glory of the widow's mite.

How much that widow's faith must have meant for her to give her all! The wealthy worshipers would have given much for the kind of faith that can trust God so completely. It is the kind of faith that is confident: "If I do my utmost, I know he will do his." The rich man accomplishes more materially for the world. The widow did more spiritually. We need great people more than we need great buildings.

⸺ Waste and Want
John 6:3-13

> When they had eaten their fill, he told his disciples,
> "Gather up the fragments left over, that nothing may
> be lost."

When I was a child and failed to eat the food that was placed before me, my mother used to quote an old proverb, "Willful waste makes woeful want." When I was old enough to know the meaning of the words I thought it meant that, if I wasted food, someday I would be in want. Now that I have become a man I know that the proverb is not so simply explained. Those who do the wasting are usually not those who do the wanting.

The food that I cast aside could mean the difference between life and death to some hungry child halfway around the world whom I may never see. The careless wasting of resources in this generation might well mean hardship to generations yet unborn. "The earth is the Lord's and the fulness thereof. . . ." Too often we act as if we have more claim upon it than the others.

What father is there who would not teach his sons and daughters, by punishment and deprivation if necessary, not to be selfish children who grab more than their share or carelessly waste what others need? Is our heavenly Father less wise? In a world that can produce enough that no child needs to go to bed hungry, how long can we fail to use our amazing ingenuity, our peak-of-creation intellects, our highest spiritual insights, all priceless gifts of God, to devise some means of feeding all of God's children? Or will we use them to fill space with our toys of destructive waste?

✓ Pleased to Give
Romans 15:24-33

> . . . I am going to Jerusalem with aid for the saints. For Macedonia and Achaia have been pleased to make some contribution for the poor. . . .

The letter which Paul wrote to his Christian friends in Rome contains some of the most profound statements of his Christian theology. Our powers of thought are strained to the utmost to comprehend them, and the Christians of the first century must have had to struggle just as much.

But the great apostle could be as intensely practical as he could be spiritually and intellectually profound. The Christian faith is never either-or. Paul wanted Christians to grapple with ideas of God so infinite in scope that they would never lose their awe and sense of mystery, but he also wanted them to live lives so practical and useful that the church would be not an "esoteric circle" but a fellowship of joyous serving.

Christians in Jerusalem were facing the tribulation and need that is always born out of discrimination. They were regarded as the misfits of their time, and every man's hand was turned against them. But their brethren in Greece, more richly blessed, rejoiced in the opportunity to minister to another's need. The people of the churches in Macedonia and Achaia were not only willing to help but "pleased to make some contribution." The Christian does not "give until it hurts"; he gives until he finds the true joy of sharing.

✓ A Lesson in Appreciation
2 Samuel 23:13-17

> "O that some one would give me water to drink from the well of Bethlehem which is by the gate!"

The mighty King David had been born and reared in the

little town of Bethlehem. When he was a man at the height of his career, at war with the Philistines, the traditional enemies of the Hebrews, he found himself besieged in the cave of Adullam. Possibly he was feeling low because of the recent problems of the conflict. In his moment of desperation, his mind went back across the years to boyhood. He remembered the cool water of the well at the gate of Bethlehem. His thoughts broke into words, "O that some person would give me a drink from that wonderful old well!"

I wonder if he fully appreciated the good gift of that water when he was a lad and could stop there anytime to quench his thirst. Often we have at hand those things which we take for granted to such an extent that we fail in gratitude. The time may come when, looking back across the years, we shall long for that which now we hold too lightly.

Perhaps David did not realize that anyone heard of his wish. At any rate, three brave men went that night, at the risk of their lives, through the enemy lines to bring back to David a drink of the water from the well at Bethlehem. Now David knew the meaning of appreciation. He took the gift with humble thanks, but, as he thought of such devotion, he could not drink it. He poured it reverently upon the ground as a gift of which only God was worthy.

+ Cut Rate Religion
2 Samuel 24:18-25

". . . I will buy it of you for a price; I will not offer burnt offerings to the Lord my God which cost me nothing."

"I can get it for you wholesale" is music to the ears of a generation plagued with the high cost of living and confused by the constant inflation of cost without respect to value. But true value cannot be inflated or deflated, and there are no "wholesale" prices.

Love cannot be bought or sold. By careful cultivation and

lavish expenditure one may win the appreciation and affection of another to the extent that love seems to exist. If and when that affection and appreciation are replaced by love, it will come and will remain without respect to material price. One cannot obtain love on a "minimum basis" or at "cut rates." The great intangibles of life—hope, character, understanding— are not on the open market; they cannot be bought or sold.

So it is with the profound relationship between God and men which we call religion. Religion has its material manifestations. A gaunt cross reminds us of a gift beyond the possibility of appraisal. The shadowed arches of a stately church localize a relationship so vast we cannot pin it down. A bit of money dropped upon an offering plate symbolizes a bit of life devoted to God. We use material symbols to try to make clear a bond of the spirit that is beyond words and symbols. But words and symbols, and, above all, the relationship, must be our own, bought with a price of our own spending. There is no "cut rate" religion. We cannot offer to God anything meaningful that costs us nothing.

— Concerning the Contribution
I Corinthians 16:1-9

> Now concerning the contribution for the saints: as I directed the churches of Galatia, so you also are to do.

Receiving an offering is not a new development for Christians. It was part of the structure of the Christian fellowship from the very beginning.

Jesus of Nazareth is the heart and soul of the church, but Paul became its mind. Jesus gave the basic principles, attitudes, and spirit of Christian teaching; nay, he was and is the primary element of that teaching. Paul laid the foundations for a Christian theology. He gave the "news behind the news," the "why" behind the "what."

Paul was also practical in the midst of all his theology and metaphysics. In this passage of Scripture, Paul has just completed a deep probing of the mystery of death. He has taken his readers beyond the bounds of earth, above the limits of life, to place them in triumph outside the reach of sin and death. But he returns to earth with a thud. "Now concerning the contribution for the saints—" he says.

He treats the Christians at Corinth as Jesus treated the disciples on the Mount of Transfiguration. It is wonderful to stand above and beyond the world with the victorious Christ, but heights are not reached by talking about them or meditating upon them. One travels a long road of shared experience to be identified with a Master who never stopped sharing. That is the reason for the sudden switch from the glory ahead to the present responsibility for hungry Christians in Jerusalem. Therefore, "On the first day of every week, each of you is to put something aside. . . ."

HOME AND FAMILY

$\left(+\right)$ Family Ties
Matthew 12:46-50

"Whoever does the will of my Father in heaven is my brother, and sister, and mother."

We sometimes quote the proverb, "Blood is stronger than water," to indicate that the family tie of common blood is the strongest tie in the world. In our Scripture lesson above, Jesus indicates that mankind has a relationship stronger than blood.

When Jesus asked, "Who is my mother, and who are my brothers?" he did not repudiate the bonds that bind a family together. Actually, he placed them on a higher level than ever before. He recognized that a family is made one, not by an accident of birth, but by a community of interest, concern, and purpose.

We know the obligations parents have to their children, but all of us have known worthy parents whose children, in spite of every effort on the part of father and mother, have proved unworthy. It seems right to recommend to children the commandment, "Honor thy father and mother," but we have also known parents who have shown themselves undeserving of honor.

Jesus gave the clue to true family unity. A family becomes a true family when the children do not owe a debt to parents, nor parents to their children, but when both recognize their debt to Someone bigger than the family. A family knows unity when it is joined in a purpose great enough that nothing else matters.

There is something further in this affirmation of Jesus. The family is always enriched by the willing adoption of others into the family circle. We should find joy in the knowledge that we live in a world where all people, whatever their race or nationality, are potentially brothers and sisters. Although it is taking us a very long time to come to this recognition, we do live in that kind of world. When we accept the fact, we are one with all who do our Father's will.

✓Only a Youth
Jeremiah 1:1-9

"Do not say, 'I am only a youth';
for to all to whom I send you you shall go,
and whatever I command you you shall speak.
Be not afraid of them. . . ."

We belittle ourselves too easily when we want to get out of a job. Jeremiah would not have been happy if someone else had said, "He does not know how to speak, for he is only a youth." Even "only a youth" has no good reason for escape when God has a job for him to do.

God never calls men or women to do a task for which he does not give them all they need to do it. On some occasions we attempt a job in which we do not have real conviction that God is using us. Then we have only ourselves to blame if we fail. There are other times when we know what God wants us to do, but we throttle our convictions and try to escape. "I am so busy." "I am only a youth." There is no end of excuses and no beginning of real reasons.

One man with God is a majority. You can do the job that God has for you. Dwight L. Moody is a good example of one who believed, "The world has yet to see what God can do with the man who is fully and wholly consecrated to Him." He served God as that man. So the untrained former store clerk became one of the sincere evangelists of the church.

Use as much ingenuity preparing for the task ahead as most people do finding excuses from it, and you with God can turn the world upside down. Jeremiah, only a youth, became one of the great prophets of history.

(+) A Good Start
Psalm 119:57-64

I hasten and do not delay to keep thy commandments.

Most people intend to live a good life, but some of them take quite a while to get around to it. Augustine once prayed, "O Lord, make me a Christian, but not yet." A young college graduate displayed his immaturity and lack of wisdom when he said, "I believe in all this church stuff, but I'm spending my first ten years out of college making all the money I can." Life is too brief at best and too uncertain to waste time being anything less than the best person possible.

It was a wise man who wrote, "I hasten and do not delay to keep thy commandments." The most important decisions in life are usually made while we are young enough to be essentially inexperienced. We must choose our life work. We must choose our life partner. Most of all, we must choose our life philosophy upon which all other choices are founded. Because we cannot depend upon our own experience in these important matters, it is good to learn to take directions and to follow a few commands. This is what youth resents most of all, and all of us revolt at least a little bit.

What we think of as the wisdom of God is that which has been tried and trusted by countless generations. It is not right because it has lasted so long, but it has lasted so long because it is right. It is a good thing to begin with a determined effort to follow the strongest lead one can discover. Life's patterns tend to become set and difficult to change. This makes it important to start right. It is always later than we think. Hasten and do not delay to keep the commandments of God

113

as they are revealed to you. Then the right pattern is the one that becomes the set and established way of life. Then what *is* is better than what *was,* and what *is to come* is best of all.

✝ Youth and Age
2 Kings 2:1-12

> . . . Elijah said to Elisha, "Ask what I shall do for you, before I am taken from you." And Elisha said, "I pray you, let me inherit a double share of your spirit."

Elijah was the greatest man in Israel in those days. Elisha must have felt highly honored to have been chosen by him and to have Elijah pay so much attention to him. Now that the end was in sight, what should Elisha seek as a final boon?

Certainly there were many things a young man might desire from so great and powerful a leader. But Elisha was an unusual young man. He was sufficiently keen to recognize that the greatest gift he could have was a good portion of that indomitable spirit that motivated Elijah.

Wouldn't it be wonderful if such spiritual gifts were transferable in our time! Do you suppose we would have enough insight to appreciate them?

But there is another side to this incident. If young Elisha found so much to be desired in Elijah, what a wonderful old man he must have been! The clash between generations is never one-sided. If we are young and resentful of the domination of elders, we may be blind to the good they have to offer. If we are old and critical of youth's lack of appreciation, perhaps we have not given them enough of the right things to appreciate. Youth and age can live together if both are moved by the right spirit.

— Indulgent Parents
I Samuel 3:10-18

". . . his sons were blaspheming God, and he did not restrain them."

What a job it is to be a good parent! One finds himself torn in the endless effort of trying to know when to restrain, when to control, when to guide, and when to let go. A child is a person and not a possession. He has his own life to live, his own decisions to make, his own benefits to secure, his own consequences to accept.

But no parent worthy of the name can or should stand idly by and let his child make wrong decisions, seek false values, or face needless consequences. The child who wishes that he could be as good as his father or mother is really dodging the issue. He can be better than his parent, and must be, or the race slips inevitably backward. However, he can best achieve that improvement over the previous generation by getting the head start of learning from his parents' experience.

The conflict between generations is always present, but it is aggravated and exaggerated from time to time. The parent will often be rebuffed as he tries to help. The child will constantly declare his independence even when he is aware of the fact that he needs the parents' help. Neither can afford to let the conflict discourage the cooperative effort.

Maybe Eli tried to restrain his boys and gave up in despair. Maybe he indulged them too much, as modern parents sometimes do with the easy assumption that the children should be permitted the things that the parents once desired but were not allowed. At any rate, the sons of Eli, who could have become leaders, became problems because Eli "did not restrain them."

— Pampered Children
Genesis 37:2-4, 12-24

> Now Israel loved Joseph more than any other of his
> children, because he was the son of his old age.

The young Joseph must have been difficult to get along with.
He had been so pampered by his father that he had an unduly
exalted opinion of himself. Even though he considered himself better than his brothers, he did not have to tell them
about it. One can understand how they came to hate him.

But Jacob, the aged father, also had responsibility in the
matter. Favoritism and partiality in a family are always disastrous. The real tragedy in the ancient story is not the potential danger or the ultimate enslavement of Joseph. The real
tragedy is the dissolution of a family, the alienation of brothers
who could have loved each other.

In Jacob's mistaken love of Joseph lay the seeds for the
destruction of a lad who showed much promise. A boy who
could have been the most popular of the brothers was inflated to a self-destroying conceit that turned his own brothers
against him. Jacob's would-be love accomplished an act that
could be matched only by hate.

But Joseph was not the only one destroyed. The other sons,
who got on reasonably well among themselves, might have
included Joseph in other circumstances. Their father's unfair-
ness changed their potential brotherliness into bitterness.

∠ God Is Waiting
Luke 15:11-24

> When he came to himself he said, ". . . I will arise and
> go to my father, and I will say to him, 'Father, I have
> sinned. . . .' "

Do we have to strike bottom before we come to ourselves?

What anguish and heartbreak might be saved if we could see ourselves as others see us!

"Prodigal" means wasteful and extravagant. That exactly described the younger son. He tossed aside the possibilities of the happiness of home as carelessly as a child might drop a scribbled page into the wastebasket. He turned his back upon the loving thoughtfulness of his father as thoughtlessly as if love were easy to discover. Least important of all, he spent his money as extravagantly as if his resources were without limit. Most important of all, he wasted precious days and weeks of life.

When he was homesick and homeless, when he was lonely for someone to love him but had no money with which to buy love, when the excitement of the first days of escape was past and he had to feed pigs, he came to himself. For such a lad, even a pig had a lesson to teach.

Jesus did not make the prodigal son the hero of the story. His degradation was not the point. It would have made his story a best seller if it were told in full detail in our time. The loving father was the hero. Patient in his heartbreak, he could wait until the boy grew up.

God is like that, and waits for you!

HOLY DAYS
AND HOLIDAYS

The New Road
Joshua 3:1-17

> ". . . you have not passed this way before. . . . you shall
> know that the living God is among you. . . ."

Joshua was the new leader of the children of Israel, now that
Moses was dead. The new leader had a new road to follow
as he led his people into the land that had been promised to
them. One could readily understand any timidity that might
be in the hearts and minds of this wandering multitude and
their untried guide.

There is a note of caution in Joshua's warning. "You have
not passed this way before." But the unpredictable Israelites
had a sure guide as they stepped out on the road. The Ark
of the Covenant, the symbol of the guidance and the goodness
of God, went before them. The fear of a strange path was
taken away because they were reassured by the presence of
a familiar guide.

A new year is before us with all its possibilities and uncertainties. We, too, have not passed this way before. On the
ancient maps of the world it was the custom of mapmakers
to write on unknown areas, "Here be dragons" or "Here be
demons."

Sir John Franklin, while going over one of these ancient
maps, crossed out the superstitious notes and wrote "Here is
God." We know our guide, for through all our years we have
been aware that the living God is among us. Why fear the
unknown road when one can depend upon the direction of
the known God?

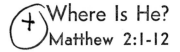

Where Is He?
Matthew 2:1-12

> "Where is he who was born king of the Jews? For we have seen his star in the East, and have come to worship him."

Modern America sings about the Twelve Days of Christmas, but loses interest in the Christ of Christmas when the rush and bustle, the giving and receiving, the lights and music are past. Epiphany is a holy day that is older than Christmas. It has been called Twelfth Night or the Twelfth Day of Christmas. Liturgical churches use the name "Epiphany" for the day on which God "revealed" himself through Jesus Christ.

Tradition has it that this is the day when wise men from a far country arrived to offer their gifts to the Christ Child. The day has also been observed as the day of Jesus' baptism.

That journey of the wise men must have been long and tedious and frustrating. The temptation to turn back must have been great. Still they persevered until their quest was fulfilled, and "they fell down and worshiped him." To worship means to recognize supreme worth. No distraction could turn them aside until they offered their choicest gifts to the One most worthy. Too often we lose interest in the Christ in the course of twelve short days of Christmas. God, as he has revealed himself in Jesus Christ, is still our supreme value—worth more than all our distractions put together.

The Big Surprise
Matthew 28:1-10

> "Do not be afraid; for I know that you seek Jesus who was crucified. He is not here; for he is risen, as he said. Come, see the place where he lay."

One of the amazing things about the Easter story is that the disciples were so surprised. Jesus had assured them several times that the evil will of man could not defeat the perfect will of God.

But are we not always like this? Good news is always too good to be true. We build up a tremendous reserve of pre-conceived notions, and we have to be shown to believe differently. God is always better to us than we deserve.

Easter is only one more of those experiences where the goodness of God outstrips the faith of man. Blessed are they who live in such constant expectation of the love of the Almighty that they rejoice in it instead of question it. How alert we are to challenge every misfortune that comes our way with "Why does this have to happen to me?" How seldom do we stand in humble awe before the good things that come, to ask "Why is God so good to me?" At long last the questions and doubts of the disciples were swept aside, but it took a bit of doing to convince them. When they were convinced, they went forth in a radiant faith that changed the world.

The questions that cluster around that first Easter Day have not found complete answers in nineteen hundred years. The impact of those who finally stopped asking for details and stepped out in an unfailing confidence in the limitless love of God has swept across the earth to change the thinking of men. The unexpected surplus of the glory of Easter is only a natural expression of God, who always gives more than any-one has any right to expect.

— God Acts Through You
Acts 2:1-12

> . . . the multitude came together, and they were bewil-
> dered, because each one heard them speaking in his own
> language.

The most confusing aspect of our traditional faith in the Trinity is that which deals with the concept of the Holy

Spirit. It should be the clearest part of it, because this is the point at which God touches us. The story of Pentecost has contributed to the confusion because there are elements in it that are far beyond our human comprehension. The Holy Spirit is God in action in you and me and all men, here and now and at all times and places. The idea of the Trinity was born out of the difficulty that beset Christians when they tried to define the indefinable.

Their faith was in God almighty, eternal, all wise, all loving. They were convinced beyond the shadow of doubt that God was in Jesus Christ revealing himself to the world and reconciling the world to himself. Had God, then, departed from his activity in the world, now that Jesus Christ was no longer physically present? Obviously such a notion would be entirely alien to the Christian idea of God. God was still acting as always, but he was acting through the lives of men and women. These were men and women not so perfectly committed to God's will as Jesus had been. They were, therefore, not such perfect instruments for the accomplishment of the divine purpose, but, where they were willing to be used, God would act through them.

At Pentecost God used men to share his truth in many languages. No wonder the crowd was amazed. When God acts through committed men, amazing things can happen in the world.

⌣ One Nation Under God
Psalm 33:1-22

Blessed is the nation whose God is the Lord,
the people whom he has chosen as his heritage!

"One nation under God" is the phrase by which, pledging our allegiance to the flag, we also acknowledge our faith in the Almighty. The mere repetition of the phrase does not necessarily imply that we are a "nation whose God is the

Lord." Faith in God is not a matter of words but of deeds, attitudes, and dedicated lives.

The key verse of our thinking is the one verse of the thirty-third psalm that is often quoted, but too often out of context. One needs the sweep of the whole passage to sense the impact of this single verse. "By the word of the Lord the heavens were made. . . . He gathered the waters of the sea as in a bottle. . . . The earth is full of the steadfast love of the Lord." This is the paean of praise to the glorious Creator. But this mighty and orderly God who created the whole design and plan for the universe is also the God of history. His is the plan in which the destinies of men and nations are worked out. "The Lord brings the counsels of the nations to naught. . . . The Lord looks down from heaven; he sees all the sons of men. . . . A king is not saved by his great army. . . ."

History is not simply the record of the experiments of men as they stumble onward and upward forever. It is the evidence of a divine plan working in the lives of men and nations. It is part of an eternal design in which little men and mighty empires have their place. "The nation whose God is the Lord" earnestly seeks its place in the divine pattern, not that its political aims may be realized but that God's eternal purpose may be fulfilled.

Proclaim Liberty
Leviticus 25:8-17

"And you shall hallow the fiftieth year, and proclaim liberty throughout the land to all its inhabitants. . . ."

Independence Day is named for our securing "independence" from England, but we live in a day when we know that no nation is truly independent. More than that, we are aware that no individual within a nation can claim independence. Men and women are mutually dependent on each other and responsible for each other.

Our famous Liberty Bell, enshrined in Independence Hall in Philadelphia, has carved in it a portion of our text. The inscription is "Proclaim liberty throughout all the land." It is important here, as in all Scripture, that we become aware of the context. The phrase is at the heart of a passage providing in law for the year of Jubilee. We have come to think of a "Year of Jubilee" as a time of rejoicing, but it is more than that. It is a recognition of responsibility. Land, in danger of losing its fertility, was to be left fallow to regain its goodness. Slaves were to be freed. Special admonition is given that financial dealings be conducted honestly. The prosperous were to provide for the needy. "Liberty throughout the land" was recognized as dependent upon concern for each other and the willing acceptance of the responsibilities of a good citizen.

Liberty today is not the cutting of all bonds, but the cooperation that guarantees freedom for all men. All citizens are responsible for assuring the opportunity for decent living for all members of society. Labor and management have mutual obligations. None can be truly free and happy unless there is provision for the freedom and happiness of all. "Proclaim liberty throughout the land," but remember what it costs.

✓ Someone Ought to—
Judges 9:6-15

> "Then all the trees said to the bramble, 'Come you, and reign over us.' And the bramble said to the trees, 'If in good faith you are anointing me king over you, then come and take refuge in my shade.'"

Even as early as the Book of Judges, politics had a bad reputation. Jotham's fable is the only true "fable" in Scripture. The use of pure fiction in which animals or inanimate objects carry on conversation was not a common Hebrew device. But one cannot miss what Jotham is illustrating any more than one can fail to see the obvious moral of one of Aesop's fables.

When a small man occupies a great position, he often gets an inflated view of his own importance. Who seeks refuge in the shade of the bramble save Br'er Rabbit? It is a wise bramble that faithfully does his job as a bramble and does not imagine that he is one of the cedars of Lebanon.

Does this mean that we should escape the responsibilities of public office in the excess of our humility? Indeed, humility and false humility have produced too much of such escape in our time.

To continue in the spirit of Jotham's fable, how much better off the trees would have been if the vine or the fig tree, the olive or the cedar of Lebanon, had been willing to serve as king! It is easy to ridicule our political brambles, but it requires a sense of dedication and responsibility among our "cedars of Lebanon" before they can be replaced. Let not the glory of your own task and ability blind you to the claims of public office and the need of the community. On the other hand, if you are a bramble in a useful spot, be a faithful bramble. Legend claims the lowly thistle saved Scotland by pricking the foot of an invader. An oak tree could not have done better.

✝ To Number Our Days
Psalm 90:1-17

So teach us to number our days
that we may get a heart of wisdom.

How uneven is the march of time. When we were children waiting for an exciting holiday, the days seemed to pass so very slowly that the very hands of the clock seemed to stand still. As adults, with the pressure of many tasks upon us or the dawning awareness of our mortality, the hours and days and years speed by too quickly.

Our psalm for a birthday is a good psalm to slow us down so we can make proper appraisal of "the years of our life." A small boy, writing a note of appreciation to a well-loved schoolteacher, ended his letter with the cordial wish, "and may you live all the days of your life." There is a wisdom in the little lad's benediction that is far beyond his years. Our psalm reminds us that "all the days of our life" pass too quickly. They find meaning only as we live them in proper relationship to the purposes of the eternal God who has "been our dwelling place in all generations." "The work of our hands" is established only insofar as it becomes a part of God's work.

"The years of our life are threescore and ten" or many more in the amazing days in which we live, and we try to make them a part of the total pattern of eternity. When we pray, "So teach us to number our days that we may get a heart of wisdom," we are not asking God to help us to count those days as they go by, but rather to help us make them count for him.

On Taking a Census
Luke 2:1-7

> And Joseph also went up . . . to be enrolled with Mary, his betrothed, who was with child . . . and she gave birth to her first born son. . . .

I wonder whether the baby Jesus was ever counted in the census that Caesar Augustus required. I expect that a newborn babe was not regarded as important. There would be plenty of time to assess his taxes at a later date if he survived the hazards of that ancient day.

It is interesting to contemplate how little even the wisdom of the rulers of Eternal Rome knew about what really counts. They gathered their heavy taxes for the security of their empire, and they have become almost a forgotten page in a history book. The Babe grew to teach men of a kingdom that is "not of this world," and he is a permanent part of the living experience of men of goodwill around the globe. They were interested in people as assets to the empire. He was concerned with people as children of God who needed to know how much their Father loved them.

How many babies seem to be born in the middle of the night! This Babe was born in the midst of a dark night for many souls, and men remembered Malachi's prophecy that "the sun of righteousness shall rise, with healing in its wings." The empire promised its people the "Roman peace," secured by the might of armed legions and, if they would behave, "bread and the circus." The Babe had reference to other promises, "for all the promises of God find their Yes in him."

The warped notions of the ancient empire still twist the thinking of mankind; but, in the constant census of values that we must always take, let us not miss the newborn Babe who counts more than all the other values of life.

✝ What's the Difference?
Luke 2:25-38

> "Lord, now lettest thou thy servant depart in peace,
> according to thy word;
> for mine eyes have seen thy salvation. . . ."

Has Christmas made any difference to you this year? It made a big difference to all the world when first it came. It gave a convincing answer to the searching of the wise men. It brought confidence and peace into the troubled lives of common shepherds. It scared the dictator Herod to death. It gave a new life purpose to a little family from a very ordinary home in Nazareth. It satisfied all the longings of a long life in Simeon and answered the expectations of Anna. What has it done for you?

For days and weeks we prepare ourselves to observe the glorious festival of the goodness of God who, out of his infinite compassion, has reached down to meet our most desperate need. We have tried to rescue the deep significance of

God's "unspeakable gift" of Jesus Christ from the commercial violations of the meaning of Christmas, the entrenched sentimentalities, the mixed motivations of "Santa Claus," and the childish self-satisfaction of our giving and receiving. Have we kept the full meaning of the great Christmas Gift through all the distractions?

Before the candles flicker out and the melody of carols is lost, while the fragrance of the Christmas tree is still in our nostrils and the love and laughter of friends and family are all about us, let us contemplate again why all these trappings have been added.

The Babe was born that we might know that God is concerned for us. He lived that we might know what a life permeated with God is like. He died and rose that we might be certain that God's love for us has no limit. Does Christmas make any difference?

The Last Chance
Ephesians 5:6-20

> Look carefully then how you walk, not as unwise men but as wise, making the most of the time, because the days are evil.

At one point all men are equal. Whether one is a millionaire or a pauper, well educated or uneducated, a thief or an honest man, we all have twenty-four hours in every day. There is no way in which we can add to our quota and no way in which anyone can rob us at this point.

But we can rob ourselves. We can so use, or misuse, the hours of our days that precious time is wasted. This is the most irreplaceable waste of all. We scold our children if they waste food, but, by the grace of God, the good earth continues to produce more. We are shocked by the waste of money, but money is only a symbol of value. We can usually replace what has been wasted, even though it requires hard work. Time is the one commodity that can never be replaced. When we have used this minute for good or evil, it is our first and last chance.

That is why Paul admonishes Christians, "Do not be foolish, but understand what the will of the Lord is." We have no time to waste on the stupidities of evil days. Each minute is a new and precious opportunity for us to build our lives into the permanent and meaningful structure of the universe. Life becomes eternal because it partakes of eternal realities. The whims, fashions, and vices of our day have no permanent reality and are but a waste of the golden moments of eternity.